AERO-NEUROSIS

PILOTS OF THE FIRST WORLD WAR AND
THE PSYCHOLOGICAL LEGACIES OF COMBAT

AERO-NEUROSIS

PILOTS OF THE FIRST WORLD WAR AND
THE PSYCHOLOGICAL LEGACIES OF COMBAT

MARK C. WILKINS

Pen & Sword
AVIATION

First published in Great Britain in 2019 by
PEN AND SWORD AVIATION
an imprint of
Pen & Sword Books Limited
Yorkshire – Philadelphia

Copyright © Mark C. Wilkins, 2019

ISBN 978 1 52672 312 3

The right of Mark C. Wilkins to be identified as the author of this work has been asserted by her in accordance with the Copyright, Designs and Patents Act 1988.

A CIP record for this book is available from the British Library
All rights reserved. No part of this book may be reproduced or transmitted in any form or by any means, electronic or mechanical including photocopying, recording or by any information storage and retrieval system, without permission from the Publisher in writing.

Printed and bound in England by
TJ International Ltd, Padstow, Cornwall

Typeset in Times New Roman 11/13.5 by
Aura Technology and Software Services, India

Pen & Sword Books Ltd incorporates the imprints of Pen & Sword Archaeology, Atlas, Aviation, Battleground, Discovery, Family History, History, Maritime, Military, Naval, Politics, Railways, Select, Social History, Transport, True Crime, Claymore Press, Frontline Books, Leo Cooper, Praetorian Press, Remember When, Seaforth Publishing and Wharncliffe.

For a complete list of Pen and Sword titles please contact
PEN & SWORD BOOKS LTD
47 Church Street, Barnsley, South Yorkshire, S70 2AS, England
E-mail: enquiries@pen-and-sword.co.uk
Website: www.pen-and-sword.co.uk

Or

PEN & SWORD BOOKS
1950 Lawrence Rd, Havertown, PA 19083, USA
E-mail: Uspen-and-sword@casematepublishers.com
Website: www.penandswordbooks.com

Contents

Acknowledgements vi
Introduction vii

Chapter 1	Building a Mechanized Age and the Rise of Nationalism 1
Chapter 2	The Rise of Flight and Cathedrals in the Sky 8
Chapter 3	The Birth of Military Aviation 13
Chapter 4	A New Kind of Warfare 19
Chapter 5	The Immortal Ace 25
Chapter 6	Coping with the Strain; Aviation Psychiatry 29
Chapter 7	Elliott White Springs – the True War Bird 40
Chapter 8	The Slow Fuse – William Lambert 66
Chapter 9	Besting the Baron – Roy Brown 73
Chapter 10	The Conscience of a Hawk – Ernst Udet 88
Chapter 11	Edward 'Mick' Mannock – Collectivist Dogfighter 104
Chapter 12	The Unlikely Ace of Aces – Georges Guynemer 125

Conclusions 136
Bibliography 140
Notes 143
Index 159

Acknowledgments

I would like to thank the following individuals and institutions for their help in compiling this book: Russ Turner, M.D. and the doctors at Wright Patterson AFB in Dayton Ohio; Michael O'Neal, President of the League of WWI Aviation Historians; Nicholas Doyle, Reproduction Manager South Carolina Library/University of South Carolina; Ann Y. Evans, Springs Close Family Archives, The White Homestead, for her generous assistance with the personal papers of E.W. Springs; Mary M. Boyd, Georgetown County Museum; Steve Ruffin for his input and insights with regards to *Warbirds*; Dawne Dewey and Lisa P. Rickey, MA, MLIS, CA Archivist for Digital Initiatives & Outreach, Wright State University Libraries Special Collections & Archives; Professor Charles Maier, Harvard University; Al Golding, Communications Co-ordinator AHRC; Nina Hadaway, Research Manager, RAF Museum London. Finally, many thanks to Karin for all her support in this endeavour.

Introduction

The men discussed in this book grew up in different parts of the world and were raised under different socio-economic circumstances. Some grew up in small towns; others grew up in or around big cities. The context of their upbringing could be applied to countless other aviators, soldiers, and sailors. If there was a common denominator to these men, it was that each loved flying—at least initially. Their upbringing and the world to which they had become accustomed would suffer a shock when the First World War began. Men used to quiet pastoral life would suddenly be thrust into the context of full scale mechanized warfare: They would be forever changed.

In the Southern and Midwestern United States of Elliott Springs, John Grider, and William Lambert, the horrors of the Civil War and turmoil of Reconstruction had passed and were replaced with the problems of economic and racial strife in the South and West – as these United States struggled to live up to the name. In Sans Souci, John Grider grew up witnessing the twilight of plantation culture. Lambert grew up in Ironton, where the raw materials for the age of urban industrialization were harvested. In Lancaster, South Carolina Springs' father built his textile mills in the fashion that echoed the experimentation, industrialization, and economic prosperity that characterized the industrial revolution – Elliott being raised in a privileged environment of the Southern upper class that was foreign to Lambert and Grider. The Canada of Roy Brown was not too dissimilar from his American comrades – Brown's upbringing more akin to Springs than that of Grider or Lambert, as Roy's father was an affluent local merchant.

The progressivism of the late nineteenth century America – characterized by civil service reform, Prohibition, and the women's suffrage movement – found a champion in Teddy Roosevelt. 'Rough Rider' Roosevelt became president after McKinley's assassination, ushering in a new age of action, blue water diplomacy, and 'square deal' policies for the average American. Labourers lobbied for an abolition of child labour and the 8 hour working day – profits were up but unions were not far off. There was no Federal income tax yet. Public schools grew like mushrooms and railroads linked not only the coasts but many smaller towns as well. Walking through any American town the syncopated tinkling of Scott Joplin's *Maple Leaf Rag* might be heard, as others riding horses made their way to work. If you worked in a large city, you would hop off your trolley car and dodge a Ford Model T tooling along at the speed limit of 12 mph and hotfoot it to the factory or mill to punch in to the newly installed time clock. After work you could look forward to a meal of chicken pudding, roast beef, or ham depending on where you lived; potatoes and some sort of biscuit or bread. Picking a newspaper off the parlour table there is mention of two brothers from Dayton Ohio who claimed to have flown a machine of their making at someplace called Kitty Hawk, North Carolina, and were now doing the same in Europe.

In the Canterbury of Mick Mannock's England, the cosy winding streets comprised of Tudor structures nestled inside the slightly crumbling ramparts of the walled city were begun in Roman times. Were it not for fashion and a few modern contrivances, it could easily be the sixteenth or seventeenth century or earlier. The great cathedral's multiple spires rose above the densely packed town like a fantastic mountain casting its long Anglican shadow over the inhabitants and quaint structures. Life was quiet, simple, and relatively uneventful; people played music, read, and worked whatever jobs they could find. Beer was abundant as was religion – nothing quite like piety to work up a thirst. The sombre Victorian era had given way to the Edwardian Age with the turn of the century, the economy was up and there was little unemployment, although living conditions were cramped. People read a lot; the novels of H.G. Wells were popular and fuelled people's craving for new technological wonders – some were understandably frightened by them.

In the France of Georges Guynemer and his affluent family, life was easier than Mannock's. Their home of Compiègne was north of Paris and was rich with history – a place where treaties were signed, kings were crowned, the magnificent fetes of Louis XIV, Louis XV, Napoleon I, and Napoleon III had occurred. Immediately following the Franco-Prussian War of 1870-71 was a period retrospectively termed the *Belle Époque* (when compared to the horrors of the First World War) or the French Third Republic, which lasted until the outbreak of the First World War. Paris was naturally at the centre, and affluent Parisians, both old money and nouveau riches, gravitated towards new forms of light entertainment such as the Moulin Rouge. For the Parisian middle class, entertainment was provided

INTRODUCTION

by cabarets, bistros and music halls. The 1889 World's Fair seemed to signal the dawn of a new and optimistic age, the crowning jewel symbolizing this new spirit was the construction of the Eiffel Tower. Its soaring iron structure seemed to point the way upward to the heavens, signalling the dawn of the aeroplane and the future. French director Georges Méliès took us on *A Trip to the Moon* in 1902, underscoring the futuristic popular mood. At around this time, a sturdy taciturn engineer named Louis Bleriot began his experiments with aircraft, as did many others.

Ernst Udet's Munich was urbane, bustling and economically robust – a reflection of the general prosperity and progress. In Germany, Kaiser Wilhelm II was building a navy to rival that of Britain. Wilhelm's fascination with the navy, and his ambition to see it as Germany's 'Blue Water Diplomacy', was reflected in everyday German life. Militarism and nationalism was on the rise; an extension of the Prussianism that resulted from the Franco-Prussian war. The distinctive spiked helmet – the so-called 'Pickelhaube' – was symbolic for the Wilhelmine period, for the Imperial army, and German militarism in general. Attitudes were rigidly conservative and Germans felt (as did the French and other European nations) that their country's influence was on the wane. The Social Democratic Party steadily grew in strength and became the largest faction in the Reichstag parliament by the 1912 elections – this party was characterized by strong loyalty towards Emperor and Reich which was condemned as revisionist and resulted in a policy of loans to fund the German war effort. In 1901, the first gasoline-powered Mercedes rolled off the line, one of the lightest, most powerful, and technically advanced of its day. In November of 1905, Albert Einstein's theory of Special Relativity was the latest ground-breaking discovery from the precocious 26-year-old scientist. The German states had an educational system which was admired and imitated elsewhere. Research at its universities was second to none in terms of quality and quantity and ambitious academics abroad actually had to learn German in order to keep up with developments in their respective subjects. By 1910, more than half of Germany's citizens lived in cities, the Udets among them. By 1914, Germany was second only to the United States as the largest industrial power in the world.

The young men in this book who flew and fought had no idea of what was awaiting them at the Western Front. The 'technology shock' that coalesced in and over France was not envisaged by any of the leadership. These men did the best they could and gave their full measure, but it was not enough. Each suffered from his experiences; some more than others. Each knew it was a defining moment in his life, never to be repeated. Many would feel that the dynamic context of aerial combat was something that, after the war, they still longed for, with all the attendant horror and exhilaration that was best experienced in the summer of their lives.

The medical and psychiatric profession evolved symbiotically with the war. Like the patients they were charged with treating, they were not prepared for what awaited them. Doctors argued over best practice for treatment, but they also had an agenda to contend with; the military, which wanted these men to return to duty as quickly as possible. With mounting casualties, each country needed every man. Aviation psychiatry was a special subset of the field as 'the troubles peculiar to flying people', as Captain Roy Brown put it, came to the fore. Terms such as aero-neurosis were coined to provide the necessary label yet, like 'shell shock', it was an inadequate term to describe the full and complete horror which overwhelmed an average psyche, especially one that was used to quiet rural life. Interestingly, Ernst Udet seems to have fared the best of those studied in this book; he came from an urban environment and faced his fears in a forthright and open manner. Finally, we are fortunate that many of these fliers chose to write books about their experiences after the war. They are an invaluable record, and perhaps more importantly were a means for many to heal. We know Elliott Spring's doctor made this observation with regards to his writing efforts. It could be termed one of the earliest forms of art therapy for war trauma – before such terms and phenomenon existed.

I am an historian and not a psychologist or psychiatrist. I find the psychology undergirding historical events fascinating and of chief interest. My objective in this book was to match expert testimony and medical opinions of the time as closely as possible with the case studies included where applicable. That being said, I do not believe that for most of the trauma experienced by these flyers, a cure of any type existed, then or now. The experience of killing other human beings is just too profoundly life-changing, compelling them to incorporate their suffering and experiences into their post-war lives as best they could.

Chapter 1

Building a Mechanized Age and the Rise of Nationalism

The late nineteenth and first decade of twentieth century America saw rapid advances in technology and the people of the world were in awe of man's ingenuity. Clean burning electric lights spread through the cities, chasing candles and kerosene lamps to rural areas for a time. Wireless telegraphy made instant communication possible; recordings of music could be heard via phonograph and the first telephone calls were made. When Kodak's Brownie camera hit the market in 1900, selling for $1, it launched over 100 years of consumer photography. Edison's vacuum tube would eventually make radio possible and, several decades later, the computer. Henry Ford's assembly line techniques revolutionized not only the auto industry but all industry, as now every product imaginable could potentially be mass produced efficiently, driving prices down and sidelining centuries of specialized artisans. By around 1915, Glenn Curtiss was mass producing the JN series of biplanes; they had already been doing this in England and Europe although it is difficult to ascertain if assembly line techniques were used.

James Beard introduced his somewhat dubious theory of 'neurasthenia' in the late nineteenth century claiming that 'The chief and primary cause of this...very rapid increase of nervousness is modern civilization, which is distinguished from the ancient by these five characteristics: steam-power, the periodical press, the telegraph, the sciences, and the mental activity of women'.[1] Beard's theories attempted to codify the effect of a rapidly urbanizing and industrializing society on the average nervous system. His writings seem to mourn the loss of the rural and agrarian lifestyle that was prevalent in pre-industrial America. In the midst of the scientific progress at the turn of the century, the seeds of war grew symbiotically as seemingly benign invention always bore the shadow of military application. Perhaps the most effective weapons to emerge from the First World War were the aeroplane, the U-boat, and the machine gun, although all of them had a longer history.

Hiram Maxim was originally from Maine, but by 1889 had become a naturalized British citizen, being knighted in 1901. He experimented with everything from electric light bulbs, coffee roasting, chemical compounds to aeroplanes, but his name will forever be inextricably tied to his crowning, albeit insidious, invention; the machine gun. After being knocked to the ground from the recoil of a rifle as a young man, Maxim realized that the energy contained in the recoil could be harnessed – this would eventually lead to his reciprocating firing pin mechanism.[2] In 1882, Maxim met an acquaintance from the US who said:

> 'Hang your chemistry and electricity! If you want to make a pile of money, invent something that will enable these Europeans to cut each other's throats with greater facility.'[3]

The following is Maxim's description of the genesis of the machine gun:

> 'It was necessary to make a series of experiments before I could make a working drawing of the gun, so I first made an apparatus that enabled me to determine the force and character of the recoil, and find out the distance that the barrel ought to be allowed to recoil in order to do the necessary work. All the parts were adjustable, and when I had moved everything about so as to produce the maximum result, I placed six cartridges in the apparatus, pulled the trigger, and they all went off in about half a second. I was delighted. I saw certain success ahead, so I worked day and night on my drawings until they were finished and went into the shop and worked myself until I had made a gun.'[4]

According to Maxim, this gun 'was a daisy', and he began showing it to key individuals in England, among them General Wolseley who, after seeing the gun, exclaimed, 'the Yankees beat all creation; there seems to be no limit to what they are able to do'. He noted that before long someone would turn out a machine that would manufacture 'full-grown men and women'.[5] Perhaps Wolseley realized the destructive power of the Maxim gun and made his comment accordingly. Presently all of London knew of the gun, including the Duke of Cambridge, commander in chief of the British army. Maxim recalled this fateful meeting:

BUILDING A MECHANIZED AGE

'"Come with me, Maxim, I will introduce you to everyone here who is worth knowing," and he did. There were several members of the Royal family present. It is needless to say that this introduction did me a lot of good. There never was a nicer man on this planet than the old and patriotic Duke of Cambridge.'[6]

Maxim demonstrated his invention all across Europe and the Middle East, spreading the virulent infection of mass destruction with delighted impunity, as he myopically worried over sales and patent rights. In a conversation with Lord Wolseley Maxim was asked if the gun could be made with an increased range with what amounted to an armour piercing shell. Maxim replied:

'Such a gun would not be so effective as the smaller gun in stopping the mad rush of savages, because it would not fire so many rounds in a minute, and that there was no necessity to have anything larger than the service cartridge to kill a man.'[7]

It is interesting how Maxim made the assumption that the gun would be used on savages not 'civilized' westerners!

Orders for the gun were placed by the French, British, Russian and German armies. There were some who saw the gun for what it was and represented. Chinese general and diplomat Li Hung Chang visited Maxim in England. After demonstrating the gun Chang commented 'This gun fires altogether too fast for China'.[8] In Constantinople Maxim was labelled 'The State of Maine Yankee with no civilized vice,' as Maxim abstained from many indulgences. One official said, 'Hang your guns, we don't want guns. Invent a new vice for us and we will receive you with open arms; that is what we want.'[9]

The key indicator for the potential of Maxim's invention should have been the battle of Omdurman, where the British army triumphed over the Arabs of the Sudan. Here, the tactical efficacy and horror of the 'killing machine' was put to the test:

'...and by far the greatest battle of all, Omdurman, there was no jamming, and the newspaper reports stated that as the Maxim gun was turned round over the plain. "A visible wave of death swept over the advancing host." The Arabs were defeated and the war ended. Sir Edward Arnold, in writing of this battle, said: "In most of our wars it has been the dash, the skill, and the bravery of our officers and men that have won the day, but in this case the battle was won by a quiet scientific gentleman living down in Kent."'[10]

Maxim, a long-time sufferer of bronchitis, patented and manufactured a pocket menthol inhaler and a larger 'Pipe of Peace', a steam inhaler using pine vapour, that he claimed could relieve asthma, tinnitus, hay fever and catarrh. After being criticized for applying his talents to quackery, he protested that 'it will be seen that it is a very creditable thing to invent a killing machine, and nothing less than a disgrace to invent an apparatus to prevent human suffering'.[11] It would appear that Maxim, in spite of the riches he garnered with his machine gun, suffered from a guilty conscience:

> 'I suppose I shall have to stand the disgrace [from inventing his inhaler] which is said to be sufficiently great to wipe out all the credit that I might have had for inventing killing machines.'[12]

This was the last line in his autobiography; after creating his insidious 'killing machine', and through his demonstrations had made it somewhat ubiquitous, he wanted ultimately to be known for his invention of a device that helped people. The Maxim gun was used by both sides during the First World War and accounted for slaughter on a grand scale when paired with the tactics reminiscent of the Napoleonic wars.

Maxim also experimented with aircraft and was not alone. Samuel P. Langley, Octave Chanute, Santos Dumont all worked to develop practical flying machines. In Dayton, Ohio, two taciturn brothers worked feverishly and secretively to perfect their own flying machine. Others raised families, contributed to their communities, danced and enjoyed life. The Wright Brothers sacrificed any semblance of a 'normal life' to pursue their singular fixation – conquering the problem of powered flight. Implicit in their partnership was the understanding that 'the only marriage they would have would be with one another'.[13] Through the fruits of their labours, they would gain admission, as well as any who bought their machines, to the skies. Their efforts finally paid off in 1904 when the Wright Model B actually broke from the sandy dunes of Kill Devil Hills, South Carolina and become the world's first practical flying machine, one that flew under its own power and most importantly could be controlled. Seemingly the Wrights were more concerned with capturing their flight on film for their patent application, than they were about making headlines with their achievement.

Fritz Haber was the German inventor of the synthesis of ammonia from its elements, which revolutionized the chemical industry and, through its use in the production of fertilizers, provided 'bread from air' for billions of people.[14] At the outbreak of the war, Haber perverted his use of the ammonia synthesis in producing 'gunpowder from air'. His rationale for the creation of poison gas was 'In peace for mankind, in war for the fatherland!'[15]

Submarines had been around since Bushnell's turtle in 1775. In 1870, Jules Verne's *20,000 Leagues Under the Sea* envisaged a modern submarine, whose tortured Captain Nemo preyed on merchant shipping and seemed to presage the modern age. By 1914, England, France, Germany, and the United States all possessed submarines. The question was always what would be their use in modern warfare? Former Prime Minister A.J. Balfour in a letter to Admiral of the Fleet, Lord 'Jackie' Fisher, dated 6 May 1913, wrote:

> 'The thing that really troubles me is not whether our submarines could render the enemy's position intolerable, but whether their submarines could render our position intolerable.'[16]

Fisher replied with a letter to Winston Churchill, First Lord of the Admiralty, in which he said that an enemy submarine is compelled to sink its victims. He continued:

> 'This submarine menace is a truly terrible threat for British commerce...it is freely acknowledged to be an altogether barbarous method of warfare...[but]the essence of war is violence, and moderation in war is imbecility.'[17]

Churchill and the Sea Lords were appalled by Fisher's letter, the consensus being that no civilized nation could condone torpedoing of unarmed merchant vessels. It was this sentiment that would ultimately draw the United States into the war in 1917.

In 1903, H.G. Wells wrote *The Land Ironclads* in which he foretold the use of the tank thirteen years before one was built, to overwhelm an entrenched foe with massive artillery support. The tank Wells described was not tracked but had pedrail wheels, a system that would be used by artillery pieces such as the German long-range gun, Big Bertha. French Captain Leon R. Levavasseur began exploring the idea for a motorized,

AERO-NEUROSIS

tracked cannon in 1903. His design called for a vehicle with a crew of three, a 75mm gun and a 80hp engine. By 1908, his design was shelved as French military leadership decided there was no need for such a weapon.

In England and Europe, undergirding the apparent prosperity and luminescent accomplishments of late nineteenth and early twentieth centuries, was a complex and personality-driven system of alliances, treaties, and understandings that kept European hegemony in check but it was strained and uneasy. Each nation felt as though its influence and importance was on the wane. Colonial projects in Africa distracted European powers/empires from ambitions in their own back yard. Most of the leadership in Europe and England were related by blood or marriage and all had a great pride in their own territorial scope, cultural history and political and economic influence. In short, nationalism was on the rise, threatening the stability of the old empires. Through the lens of restoring national greatness war was perceived as a viable solution. A lively and poetic description of the situation is found in the work of H.G. Wells, who presciently wrote in 1908 about the rise of nationalism in Europe:

> 'Of all the productions of the human imagination that make the world in which Mr. Bert Smallways lived confusingly wonderful, there was none quite so strange, so headlong and disturbing, so noisy and persuasive and dangerous, as the modernizations of patriotism produced by imperial and international politics. In the soul of all men is a liking for kind, a pride in one's own atmosphere, a tenderness for one's Mother speech and one's familiar land.'[18]

Wells continued his idealistic and aspirational discourse blaming the rapid trajectory and scope of science and calling for the need for a 'reasonable synthesis' of power in Europe, pre-dating the idea for a League of Nations well before Woodrow Wilson was even President:

> '... the age that blundered at last into the catastrophe of the War in the Air – was a very simple one, if only people had had the intelligence to be simple about it. The development of Science had altered the scale of human affairs. By means of rapid mechanical traction, it had brought men nearer together, so much nearer socially, economically, physically, that the old separations into nations and kingdoms were no longer possible,

a newer, wider synthesis was not only needed, but imperatively demanded. Just as the once independent dukedoms of France had to fuse into a nation, so now the nations had to adapt themselves to a wider coalescence, they had to keep what was precious and possible, and concede what was obsolete and dangerous. A saner world would have perceived this patent need for a reasonable synthesis, would have discussed it temperately, achieved and gone on to organize the great civilization that was manifestly possible to mankind.'[19]

On the night of 14-15 April 1912, man's crowning technological achievement and 'triumph over nature' slid quietly under a flat calm North Atlantic after striking an iceberg. In 2 hours and 20 minutes some 1,500 people had perished with it. The sinking of the RMS *Titanic* more than anything else seemed to signal the dawn of the modern age. In another year, Woodrow Wilson was elected and instituted the first permanent federal income tax, summarily driving in the final coffin nail on the Gilded Age in the United States. The following year Franz Ferdinand and his wife Sophie were assassinated in Sarajevo – the match that set Europe on fire. Later that fateful summer, the world was at war in a way it never could have imagined, as British Foreign Secretary Edward Grey presciently stated on the eve of war, 'The lamps are going out all over Europe; we shall not see them lit again in our life-time'.[20]

Chapter 2

The Rise of Flight and Cathedrals in the Sky

Flying was perhaps the most exciting, the most mesmerizing and magical experience of the early twentieth century. Nothing else came close and the same could be said of today. For centuries, man had dreamed of flying, of finally gaining access to the realm of the sky, or heavens, or the gods. From the late nineteenth to the early twentieth century, flight was an obsession across the entire globe. The Wrights were first to achieve powered controlled flight, which was nothing short of a miracle born out of diligence, gifted insight and persistence, but they did owe a debt to others that had worked with gliders, models, and ideas dating back to Leonardo Da Vinci. Octave Chanute, Otto Lilienthal, and others contributed ideas and observations that helped the Wrights along their lonely and self-absorbed path to success.

In Europe and to a lesser extent the United States, the age of the airplane had arrived. The following passage by H.G. Wells describes the mood and climate of the times:

> '…it was during the consequent great rise of prices, confidence, and enterprise that the revival of interest in flying occurred. It is curious how that revival began. It was like the coming of a breeze on a quiet day; nothing started it, it came. People began to talk of flying with an air of never having for one moment dropped the subject. Pictures of flying and flying machines returned to the newspapers; articles and allusions increased and multiplied in the serious magazines. People asked in mono-rail trains, "'When are we going to fly?' A new crop of inventors sprang up in a night or so like fungi. The Aero Club announced the project of a great Flying Exhibition in a large area of ground that the removal of slums in Whitechapel had rendered available.'[1]

THE RISE OF FLIGHT AND CATHEDRALS IN THE SKY

Wells' passage was written in 1908, one year before Louis Bleriot flew the Channel and the seminal Rheims Air Meet took place but the interest in aviation was viral as Wells so aptly describes. Men such as Bleriot, Santos Dumont, Garros and Voisin all were busy building, testing, and flying their machines. 1908 was also the year that the Wrights finally demonstrated their flyer at Le Mans[2] and finally secured a military contract with the U.S. Army Signal Corps (explained in chapter 4). The age of flight had finally come into being; its time had come, and those that embraced this spirit excelled quickly and readily; those who believed it belonged to one person were quickly left behind. This notion was both exemplified and ratified at the pivotal Rheims Air Meet during the summer of 1909. Bleriot's crossing of the English Channel 'captured the imagination of the masses in a way that Wilbur Wright's flights, witnessed primarily by rich and idle people had never done'.[3] During the 'Grande Semaine' at Rheims the only luminaries conspicuously absent were the Wrights. During this one meeting, every record held by the Wrights was broken in a single week. Bleriot and Glenn Curtiss seemed to dominate the meet with Curtiss winning the Gordon Bennett Prize for Speed, bettering Bleriot's time by 5.6 seconds.[4]

The realm of the heavens that had eluded man's grasp for so long was now accessible with the advent of the aeroplane. The public's mesmerized gaze now angled skywards as the lone aviator perched on his machine of canvas and wood soared through the clouds. H.G. Wells in *War in the Air* in 1908, wrote the following description of his fictitious character's (Bert Smallways) ascent in a balloon:

> 'To be alone in a balloon at a height of fourteen or fifteen thousand feet – and to that height Bert Smallways presently rose is like nothing else in human experience. It is one of the supreme things possible to man. No flying machine can ever better it. It is to pass extraordinarily out of human things. It is to be still and alone to an unprecedented degree. It is solitude without the suggestion of intervention; it is calm without a single irrelevant murmur. It is to see the sky. No sound reaches one of all the roar and jar of humanity, the air is clear and sweet beyond the thought of defilement. No bird, no insect comes so high. No wind blows ever in a balloon, no breeze rustles, for it moves with the wind and is itself a part of the atmosphere. Once started, it does not rock nor sway; you cannot feel whether it rises or falls. Bert felt acutely cold, but he wasn't

mountain-sick; he put on the coat and overcoat and gloves Butteridge had discarded--put them over the 'Desert Dervish' sheet that covered his cheap best suit--and sat very still for a long, time, overawed by the new-found quiet of the world. Above him was the light, translucent, billowing globe of shining brown oiled silk and the blazing sunlight and the great deep blue dome of the sky.'[5]

Wells' description indicates that he probably took a ride in a balloon which had a lasting effect on him, as well as fuelling his inspiration for the theme of his tract. We are fortunate when a gifted writer described what he saw aloft! Most aviators were neither poets nor talented writers so there is no way adequately to describe the emotional and aesthetic experience of flight, although many tried. Those that were gifted writers have given us an invaluable portrait of the romance of early flight. Cecil Lewis, a First World War aviator, describes the birth of a cloud while on patrol:

'I was about to turn west again when I saw, in the distance, a cloud floating above the floor, small, no bigger than a man's hand; but even as I looked, it seemed to grow. It swelled, budded, massed, and I realized I was watching the very birth of a cloud – the cumulus cloud that chiefly makes the glory of the sky, the castles, battlements, cathedrals of the heavens…a marriage of light and water, fostered by the sun, nourished by the sky! I turned towards it, fascinated. It grew rapidly. Soon it was vast, towering, magnificent, its edges sharp, seemingly solid, though constantly swelling and changing. And it was alive with light. Radiant white, satin soft, and again gold, rose-tinted, shadowed and graded into blue and mauve shadows—an orient pearl in the shell of heaven! I edged nearer. I was utterly alone in the sky yet suddenly, against the wall of the cloud, I saw another machine. It was so close that instinctively, as an instantaneous reaction to the threat of collision, I yanked the stick and reeled away, my heart in my mouth. A second later, I looked round and laughed. There was nothing there! It was my own shadow I had seen, the silhouette of the machine on the white cheek of the cloud. I came back to observe the strange and rare phenomenon. There on the cloud was my shadow, dark, clean-cut; but more

THE RISE OF FLIGHT AND CATHEDRALS IN THE SKY

than the shadow, for around it was a bright halo of light, and outside that a perfect circular rainbow, and outside that again another rainbow, fainter, reversed.'[6]

This beautiful and poetic description of the magnificence of the aerial environment is as relevant today as then. Where else could one witness such magic but from above? For centuries man has looked skyward and dreamt lazily about shapes in the clouds but importantly the viewpoint had always been the same: standing on terra firma and looking upwards. Finally, man could witness and share a completely new perspective and witness the dynamic and ever-changing skyscape of the heavens. Lewis had the following to say about the miracle of the aeroplane and flight:

> 'The wing-tips of the planes, ten feet away, suddenly caught my eye, and for a second the amazing adventures of flight overwhelmed me. Nothing between me and oblivion but a pair of light linen-covered wings and the roar of a 200 hp engine! There was the fabric, bellying slightly in the suction above the plane, the streamlined wires, taut and quivering, holding the wing structure together, the three-ply body, the array of instruments, and the slight tremor of the whole aeroplane. It was a triumph of human intelligence and skill—almost a miracle. I felt a desire to touch these things, to convince myself of their reality. On the ground they seemed strong and actual enough, but here, suspended on an apparent nothing, it was hard to believe that flying was not a fantastic dream out of which I should presently awake.'[7]

James Norman Hall, pilot of the Lafayette Escadrille and eventual co-author of *Mutiny on the Bounty*, writing a letter home discussing the rapture of learning to fly, added, 'I know, now, why birds sing'[8] – a comment he was to never live down as it became known to his squadron mates giving rise to all manner of teasing. Hall describes his final flight over the Western Front in 1918 at the time of the Armistice:

> 'What a glorious sensation it was, after six months in a prison camp, to be travelling by route of air again! I am grateful for the fact that I never became used to flying in the sense of being wearied by it. Every time I left the earth, I felt exhilarated,

AERO-NEUROSIS

lifted up in spirit as well as in body. It was, rather as though I had left my body behind, and all the slowness and heaviness of corporeal existence.'[9]

Arthur Gould Lee described his thoughts on flying above the Western Front:

'Compared with ordinary earthbound mortals, I am an Olympian God, and thrown high in the heavens, free, serene, uninvolved. Compared with the wretched millions locked in earthly combat, I and my companions are a winged aristocracy among warriors, looking down on the invisible trenches below in pity and amazement.'[10]

Writing many years later, aviation pioneer Charles Lindbergh had this to say about the reverie he experienced while flying as an airmail pilot:

'The last tint of pink disappears from the western sky, leaving to the moon complete mastery of night. Its light floods through woods and fields; reflects up from bends of rivers; shines on the silver wings of my biplane, turning them a greenish hue. It makes the earth seem more like a planet; and me a part of the heavens above it, as though I too had a right to an orbit in the sky. I look down toward the ground, at the faintly lighted farmhouse windows and distant glow of cities, wondering what acts of life are covered by the weird semidarkness in which only outlines can be seen...And all those myriad lights, all the turmoil and works of men, seem to hang so precariously on the great sphere hurtling through the heavens, a phosphorescent moss on its surface, vulnerable to the brush of a hand. I feel aloof and unattached, in the solitude of space. Why return to that moss; why submerge myself in the brick-walled human problems when all the crystal universe is mine?'[11]

Lindbergh also very wisely and astutely mentioned that poetry belongs to the novice, as he is seeing the realm of the clouds and sky with a fresh eye. With more experience comes a callousness from repetition that the beginner does not know. Military application and the war would add a new layer of wariness to flying that yielded Orville Wright's somewhat ironic comment in the following chapter.

Chapter 3

The Birth of Military Aviation

Orville Wright famously said, 'The Dream has become the Nightmare', an ironic statement considering the Wrights contributed to the escalation in viewing the aeroplane as a weapon of war. The story of the Wrights' development of their *Flyer*, and their efforts to find buyers first in the U.S., then Britain, then France, then Germany is best left to other books that deal with this subject in detail. Suffice it to say that the essential paradox with the Wrights is that their difficulty in finding a buyer stemmed from their unwillingness to demonstrate their flyer without a signed contract and the buyers were unwilling to agree to their rather high price without a demonstration! In the end, after failed negotiations in Britain, France and Germany, the US Signal Corps finally drafted a Request for Proposals (RFP) that exactly matched the Wrights' *aeroplane*. After mostly successful demonstrations at Fort Myer in August 1908, the Wrights concluded their deal with the US military on 30 July 1909. It was anti-climactic as just five days earlier Bleriot had made his historic flight across the English Channel, captivating the suddenly smaller world.

Military application of aviation began almost with the first few flights. The Wrights actively pursued the US government to purchase their flyer:

> '...by January of 1905 the Wrights and also began to think of themselves as entrepreneurs with a precious article to sell and they were keenly aware that in the increasingly militarizing conflict-ridden atmosphere of that year in France and Germany came to the brink of war the most likely clients for their invention where governments that could ill-afford to risk falling behind technologically in the race to develop ever more sophisticated and destructive engines of War.'[1]

When the US government turned them down, they felt they could proceed to foreign governments with a clear conscience.[2] How they could so quickly turn their backs on their own country is somewhat curious, especially in light of how they have come to symbolize such a distinctly American achievement in aviation historiography. However, this was a time of relative innocence with regards to the proprietary nature of military hardware.

The Wrights next offered the flyer to the British government suggesting a price of '500 pounds for each mile covered with a load of two men'. The sum was too high for the British and was compounded by the notion that the British aeronautical community thought they could produce a flying machine of their own. The Wrights next turned to France.[3]

In spite of the urging of Wilbur Road Ferber, the French War Ministry turned the Wrights down as well due to the inflated price (1 million francs).[4] These dealings abroad contributed to the image that the Wrights seemed 'provincial and eccentric but wily businessmen who were determined to keep the details of their flyer secret until it had been sold at a handsome price.'[5]

Robert Wohl wrote that:

> 'It was one of the paradoxes of the early history of Aviation that, though powered flight was first achieved in the United States, the capital of Aviation before the First World War was indisputably Paris. No other Western City prize aviators more highly, or responded to their exploits with more intense enthusiasm.'[6]

Brazilian expatriate Alberto Santos-Dumont dominated the Parisian aeronautical scene during the first six years of the twentieth century. On 12 November 1906, Dumont flew between 722 and 726 feet in his 14bis (accounts vary).[7] Lord Northcliffe, an aviation enthusiast and owner of the *Daily Mail*, was present for this flight. He read the account in the *Mail* and was extremely upset, contacting the editor to say that:

> 'The news was not that Santos-Dumont Flies 722 feet, but England is no longer an island. There will be no sleeping safely behind the wooden walls of old England with the Channel our safety moat. It means the aerial chariots of a foe descending on British soil if war comes... they are not mere dreamers who hold that the time is at hand when air power will be even more important than sea power.'[8]

THE BIRTH OF MILITARY AVIATION

The Wrights remained stubbornly secretive about their *Flyer* throughout 1906 and were convinced that there was no meaningful competition in Europe or Britain:

> 'However, when news arrived (by way of an increasingly critical Chanute) of a spectacular flight by the Brazilian Santos-Dumont in Paris the Wrights began to reconsider their tactics... But they were concerned (and rightly so) that Santos-Dumont's exploit would create a perception that controlled flight was within easy reach and thus diminish the value of their machine in the eyes of potential customers.'[9]

Becoming anxious that other aviation designers were catching up to them, they secured an arms dealer, Charles R. Flint, to try to sell their *Flyer* abroad.[10] Wilbur accompanied Flint to France; however, the French thought that Wilbur seemed more interested in profit than in glory and they believed, like the British, that France would soon produce a machine as good if not better than the Wrights' *Flyer*.

Negotiations with Flint went back and forth and the Wrights sought input from Chanute who 'asked if they had considered the moral implications of turning such a potential weapon over to a European nation'.[11] Ultimately, the Wrights did not want to give Flint & Co. a free hand in selling their aeroplane, and concentrated their efforts on selling it to the US government.[12] Orville would work on the US signal Corps at home, while Wilbur would finally make public demonstration flights in France as a way to dispel the inertia that plagued the US at this time.

In spite of Lord Northcliffe's anxieties over nascent airpower, Santos-Dumont criticized the climate in Britain regarding advances in aviation. 'You English are practical, but you don't encourage inventors or beginners. You wait to reap the fruit of other people's brains.'[13] The British military remained sceptical about investing in aircraft; they were finally swayed not by developments in France but by Count Zeppelin's flight of 240 miles in Germany using his rigid airship in July of 1908.[14] The Kaiser's government intimated their intention to construct an aerial armada even more threatening than their battleship fleet. The nightmarish vision of airships 'dripping death' above London as described by H.G. Wells was a clear case of life imitating art.

While debates and anxieties raged in London and Paris, Wilbur Wright was assembling the *Flyer* in Leon Bollee's automobile factory in Le Mans, where Wilbur Wright finally went public with his flying machine. Regarding this historic flight, the *Daily Mail* wrote:

> 'The scoffer and the sceptic are confounded ... A bird could not have shown a more complete mastery of flight.'[15]

At about the same time that Orville was preparing for tests at Fort Myer, the American army's stance towards aviation was skewed heavily towards observation. The Signal Corps was the branch of the army that entertained the notion of using the aeroplane for this purpose. Orville arrived at Ft. Myer in August 1908, where he made several successful flights that were slightly marred by a crash on 17 September in which Thomas Selfredge was killed and Orville was seriously injured.[16] He remained hospitalized for seven weeks.

Between 8 August 1908 and 2 January 1909, Wilbur made 129 flights in France establishing nine world records. Most of the flights were from Camp d'Avours, with nine being from Les Hunaudieres.[17] In December 1908, after more negotiations with the Wrights, the US Signal Corps issued an advertisement for a 'heavier-than-air flying machine' that corresponded exactly to the specifications of the (Wright) flyer and met the brothers rock-bottom demand for a price of $25,000 to be paid after a series of demonstration flights.[18] On 12 January 1909, Wilbur was joined by Katherine and Orville in Paris, where they then went south to Pau for the winter, where he made 64 flights. Pau was the winter home to the aristocracy and social elites of Europe; all were captivated by the Wrights. From here Wilbur went to Rome, and by the end of April it was time to return to the States to conclude their deal with the US army. They sailed for home on 4 May.

After the Wrights' return, the entire European aviation community had been digesting what Wilbur had shown them. Bleriot was quick to co-opt wing warping for his namesake monoplane. Others had been watching too. Santos-Dumont faded from the spotlight. Henry Farman took his place as France's premiere aviator; his ambition was simple – to fly the Channel and win the *Daily Mail* prize.[19] Other contenders were Leon Delagrange, Charles de Lambert, Louis Bleriot, and Hubert Latham.

Latham tried to cross in his Antoinette monoplane on 19 July from Calais but seven miles out his engine quit; he landed on a wave and became the first pilot to 'ditch' an aircraft. When Louis Bleriot found out, he immediately notified the *Daily Mail*'s Paris office of his intention to fly the Channel.[20]

Bleriot's experiments with aircraft began about the same time that the Wrights first went to Kitty Hawk, finally becoming airborne in his Bleriot VI in July 1907. His progress was steady but fraught with setbacks. On 13 July

THE BIRTH OF MILITARY AVIATION

1909, he flew 42 km from Etampes to Orleans in under 45 minutes winning the Aero-Club's Prix du Voyage. While Latham prepared another *Antoinette*, Bleriot had set up a camp on a small farm near the cliffs of Sangette; both men were grounded due to poor weather.[21] At 4:35 am on 25 July, Bleriot broke ground and was on his way across the Channel. 36.5 minutes later, he landed in a meadow near Dover Castle, England!

Five days later, the Wrights fulfilled their tests for the U.S. Signal Corps, coming in a better than 42.5 mph and thus earning a purchase price of $30,000.[22] Four days earlier Glenn Curtiss sold his *Golden Flier* for $5,000 to Aeronautic Society of New York,[23] thus beginning the long patent war between Curtiss and the Wrights. This first military contract awarded to the Wrights would become the prototype for all subsequent aviation contracts. It was the beginning of the long arduous marriage of aviation technologically and the military that continues to this day.

The significance of Bleriot's flight as a paradigm shift was enormous and both the French and the British were keenly aware of this. If the Channel could be crossed by aeroplane, naval influence was suddenly obsolete. The French Press took pride in the fact that the deed had been accomplished by a French Aviator using an aeroplane of French design, just as any country would with such an achievement. The *Daily News* wrote:

> '... a rather Sinister significance will no doubt be found in the presence of our great fleet at Dover just the very moment when, for the first time, a flying man passed over that sacred 'silver streak' [the Channel] and flitted far above the masts of the greatest battleship.'[24]

Bleriot was treated like a rock-star with crowds lining the boulevards to get a brief glimpse of the man who 'with a single *coup de ses ailes* (beating of his wings), had eliminated the age-old barrier of the English Channel'.[25]

Lord Northcliffe had created one of the great news stories of the time, but his end game was to use Bleriot's exploit to exert pressure on the British government to commit itself to the rapid development of an air arm.[26] The *Daily Mail* described the paradigm shift that had occurred perfectly:

> 'British insularity had vanished; expensive dreadnoughts would be useless against swarms of relatively cheap and quickly manufactured aeroplanes. Sea Power no longer Shielded against attack men and navigate the air know nothing of Frontiers and can laugh at the Blue Streak the British Navy.'[27]

AERO-NEUROSIS

Within a week of Bleriot's flight, the Liberal government's Minister of War R.B. Haldane found himself under savage parliamentary attack and what one historian has called 'the beginning of air power politics in Britain'. that result of this debate was the demand for an independent Air Service they would eventually culminate in the Royal Flying Corps and its final successor; the Royal Air Force.[28]

For France, Bleriot's feat was an affirmation of national pride. The country that had been a leader in other forms of transportation (i.e. cars, submarines, dirigibles and balloons) was now a leader in aviation. Bleriot was somewhat surprised by the reaction to his feat and had unwittingly created a 'new form of mass-spectacle: the long-distance flight'.[29]

With the outbreak of the war, few if any planes were armed; this naïve early period of military aviation was characterized by using aircraft for reconnaissance. Aircraft on each side flew serenely by one another on their way to spot for artillery, or troop movements. Young men being what they were and are, began signalling profane gestures to each other, which led a mini arms race of sorts, starting with pistols and ending up with fully integrated machine guns fastened to the airframe along the longitudinal axis of the fuselage, such that the pilot could sight down its barrel and use the entire aeroplane as a 'point and shoot' weapon.

Cecil Lewis wrote:

> 'With the exception of the Royal Aircraft Factory at Farnborough, which was a government organization, the manufacture of aircraft was then, as now a private business...Although war was a tremendous stimulus, aerodynamical data was almost non-existent. Every new machine was an experiment, obsolete in the eyes of the designer before it was completed, so feverishly and rapidly did knowledge progress...'[30]

In August 1914, Britain flew French planes; France flew Bleriot XIs; Germany flew Rumpler Taubes – this being the first plane to be 'forced down' on August 25, 1914 by three RFC No. 2 squadron of unknown type.[31]

Chapter 4

A New Kind of Warfare

'Yet (Oh, the catch at the heart!), among the devastated cottages, the tumbled, twisted trees, the desecrated cemeteries, opening, candid, to the blue heaven, the poppies were growing! Clumps of crimson poppies, thrusting out from the lips of craters, straggling in drifts between the hummocks, undaunted by the desolation, heedless of human fury and stupidity, Flanders poppies, basking in the sun!'[1]

One of the unique contexts in history was the period before the First World War; a period where the leadership thought that war was the only solution to nationalistic ambitions. There was a certain impatience that characterized the rush to war in the summer of 1914 – infrastructure did not help matters as now as never before troops could be rushed to the area of conflict via the railways. Troops, horses, ammunition, machine guns, barbed wire and, materiel were all expeditiously rushed to the Franco-Belgian border to counteract the German advance through Belgium and northern France. The Schlieffen plan itself was based on Roman tactics of encirclement – another nod to the past.

Before the outbreak of what came to be termed the First World War, the last war fought by the France and Germany was the Franco-Prussian war of 1870-1. This war was characterized by Napoleonic war tactics and strategies – frontal assaults, cavalry charges, sword play – but most importantly there was hand to hand combat; the enemy was literally right in front of you. In fact, the use of railways was the only modern aspect of this war; the Prussians had 26 rail lines as compared to a single line used by the French. Ironically, these were the same tactics employed during 1914 only this time the weaponry all but eliminated their efficacy giving rise to fixed position fighting or 'trench warfare'. Troops still made frontal assaults but now it was into machine gun fire and barbed wire being cut down like so much wheat by a seemingly invisible enemy. Joanna Bourke wrote that:

> 'it became clear that the industrialized battlefield as devised by physicists and engineers heightened rather than diminished the importance of "human factors" …time and time again, men, after their first taste of combat, confessed…that they "saw no one" and were "unnerved" by the feeling that they were "fighting phantoms."'[2]

Germany's victory over France in 1871 consolidated faith in Prussian militarism which would remain through the Second World War. Germany's annexation of Alsace-Lorraine aroused a deep longing for revenge in the French people, and the period between 1871 and 1914 was characterized by a fragile peace; as France's silent resolve to recover Alsace-Lorraine clashed with Germany's imperialist ambitions and rising militarism kept the two nations on the cusp of conflict. Their mutual animosity proved to be a driving force behind the prolonged slaughter on the Western Front in the First World War.[3]

The solution to the stalemate seemed to be ever increasing calibres and quantities of artillery culminating with monstrosities such as the German Big Bertha siege gun, a weapon that could lob a 420mm shell 7.8 miles.[4] These new and increasingly awful weapons were being churned out on both sides of the line that snaked its way across northern France and Belgium. The result was an extra-terrestrial landscape of endless shell craters and burnt twisted vestiges of what were once trees. Towns were reduced to piles of rubble. The dead and dying were everywhere, killed not by other soldiers face to face, but in a detached fashion; from a faceless enemy who manifested itself in all manner of horrific inventions.

The men in the trenches lived with never ending mud, rats, disease, malnutrition, cold, and the hopelessness resulting from the tactics and weapons employed. The following passages by Erich Remarque in his classic *All Quiet on the Western Front* evoke the feelings and mood of trench warfare:

> 'Thus we live a closed hard existence of the utmost superficiality, and rarely does an incident strike out a spark. But then unexpectedly a flame of Grievous and terrible yearning flares up. Those are the most dangerous moments. They show

us that the adjustment is only artificial, that is not simple rest, but sharp is struggle for rest... A man perceives with alarm how slight is the support, how thin the boundary that divides him from the darkness. We are little Flames poorly sheltered by frail walls against the storm of dissolution and Madness, and which we flicker and sometimes almost go out... everyday and every hour, every shell and every death cuts into this thin support, and the years waste it rapidly. I see how it is already gradually breaking down around me.'[5]

The notion of 'little flickering flames poorly sheltered by frail walls' is a compelling analogy for what men in the trenches must have felt like, as at any moment their fragile world could be decimated by an artillery shell, clouds of gas, or, as the war progressed, tanks and aeroplanes, fantastic extensions of the 'faceless enemy'. Artillery barrages left the landscape devoid of vegetation (except for poppies!), giving rise to craters pock-marked by more craters, which invariably filled with water creating a slurry of mud and blood as the following passage from *All Quiet* describes:

'The rifles are caked, the uniforms caked, everything is fluid and dissolved, the Earth One dripping, soaked, oily mass in which lie yellow pools with red spiral streams of blood into which the dead, wounded, and survivors slowly sink down.'[6]

Those in the trenches suffered from all types of new weapons, but perhaps the most insidious weapon of all was gas; Mustard, Phosgene and chlorine gases were all used during the war, courtesy of Fritz Hubert. The following passage by Cecil Lewis is both chilling and poignant:

'In the light westerly wind it slid slowly down the German trenches, creeping panther-like over the scarred earth, curling down into dugouts, coiling and uncoiling at the wind's whim. Men were dying there, under me, from a whiff of it: not dying quickly, nor even maimed or shattered, but dying whole, retching and vomiting blood and guts; and those who lived would be wrecks with seared, poisoned lungs, rotten for life. I stared at the yellow drift, hypnotized. I can see it at this moment as clearly as I could that day, for it remains with me as the most pregnant memory of the war. It was, in fact, the symbol of our enlightened twentieth century: science, in the pursuit of knowledge, being exploited by a world without standards or scruples, spiritually bankrupt.'[7]

Tanks were invented to break the stalemate and were developed under the stewardship of Winston Churchill's 'Landships Committee'. The first tank – the British Mark I – was used in battle for the first time at Flers-Courcelette on 15 September 1916.[8] Tanks had a crew of eight men 'and in addition to the fumes, the cramped conditions and the deafening noise, it was virtually pitch black inside the Mark I when going into action. Every door, flap and hatch were shut tight against bullets, shrapnel and bullet 'splash', yet the crew had to be able to see outside both to drive and fight. At the Front, the commander and his driver had large flaps that could be opened in layered stages as required, and slim periscopes which poked up through holes in the cab roof. Elsewhere in the tank were narrow vision slits with crude periscopes which used shatterproof strips of shiny steel rather than glass blocks.

German troops soon learned to fire at the tank's vision devices, which the crews tried to camouflage with paint. Other apertures, covered by teardrop-shaped flaps, were designed not for vision but to allow crew members to use their revolvers.

Cecil Lewis condemned the entire scientific community—blaming science for all the slaughter endemic of the First World War and turning a blind eye to the leadership who wielded these horrible weapons:

> 'For intellectually, the problem is not insoluble, though it is vast and has been rushed on us in under a hundred years, that is, practically instantaneously. Science is the first cause; but scientists wash their hands of it, saying they are bound to advance knowledge, but cannot control the uses men put it to. But if there is to be any safety in the world, dangerous inventions will have to be protected as carefully as dangerous poisons. To nearly every modern problem there is an intellectual answer; but that, unfortunately is not enough, for we have passions as well as minds, and they are more difficult to educate.'[9]

It is unfair to saddle the scientific community with the burden of blame for how their inventions were used, as the leadership that implemented these weaponized devices, compounds, etc. had the final say as to their use.

A NEW KIND OF WARFARE

Still, as described in chapter one there was an insular, almost child-like fascination with man's ingenuity in spite of its implicit horror. It is true that had more thought gone into 'should we' rather than the pursuit of 'can we' many of these weapons would have stayed safely in the darkest corners of human imagination.

The following passage is an excerpt from a description written in 1914 of the interior of German U-boat U9 by Johannes Speiss, First Watch Officer of U9:

> 'Then came the Commanding Officer's cabin, fitted with only a small bunk and clothes closet, no desk being furnished. Whenever a torpedo had to be loaded forward or the tube prepared for a shot, both the Warrant Officers' and Commanding Officers' cabins had to be completely cleared out. Bunks and clothes cabinets then had to be moved into the adjacent officers' compartment, which was no light task owing to the lack of space in the latter compartment…In order to live at all in the officers' compartments a certain degree of finesse was required. The Watch Officer's bunk was too small to permit him to lie on his back. He was forced to lie on one side and then, being wedged between the bulkhead to the right and the clothes-press on the left, to hold fast against the movements of the boat in a seaway. The occupant of the berth could not sleep with his feet aft as there was an electric fuse-box in the way. At times the cover of this box sprang open and it was all too easy to cause a short circuit by touching this with the feet.'[10]

As the war progressed, a term came to be coined to describe the epic carnage and fury of these new and horrible weapons; 'brutalization.' This term comes closer to the mark in describing the character of this war than the ubiquitous 'Shell-shock' which will be discussed in chapter 6. This brutalization occurred on multiple levels: Firstly, the physicality of the bodies of men being torn apart by artillery rounds, barbed wire, machine guns, and gas. Secondly, there was the brutalization of the human psyche, the effect of these new and highly mechanized and terrifying weapons that wore the mask of iron and steel; or the 'panther-like' vapour of gas as described by Lewis, his most lasting and poignant characterization of the war. In the air, the prophesies of H.G. Wells and Jules Verne seem to have materialized, the sky being darkened by warplanes and zeppelins raining death down from above; a completely new and utterly terrifying phenomenon, for who can hide from aerial bombardment? The Great War saw the quest by every nation for the decisive weapon, born from the writings of the nineteenth century military theorist Carl von Clausewitz, who argued that this was the only way to win a war. This in turn yielded the dark corollary that if something was available – like poison gas – it should be used.

While those in the trenches suffered greatly from mechanized warfare, those above also suffered from the effects of combat flying, a completely new and untried phenomenon that was advancing on a daily basis. It did have one thing in common with trench warfare; the enemy was using a machine to conduct war. On the other hand, the enemy was evenly matched, one to one. Three separate and interdependent areas emerged simultaneously during the war in the air from 1914-1918: aircraft design; combat tactics and piloting; and aviation psychiatry. Each was distinctly different, progressed rapidly, and influenced one another. For example, the early slow-moving, lightly armed, frail aircraft were a completely different animal from the fast flying rugged gun platforms of the later war. Men's nervous systems and psyches struggled to keep up with the rapid advances and increased mortality rates as the war in the air became as increasingly mechanized as the war on the ground. The chief difference was that in the air, combat was one to one usually, as opposed to the indiscriminate slaughter on the ground due to epic artillery barrages from which there was no escape. This new and terrifying phenomenon gave added credence to the prescient writings of H.G. Wells and others in the literary sphere, that a new and dreadful age was upon us, one that was hierarchical, with the human subordinate to the machine. It was the dawn of a new and frightening mechanized age that had a momentum and trajectory of its own making.

Chapter 5

The Immortal Ace

> 'I zoom up violently, the pressure pushes me into my seat, my sight goes for a second, then more shots, they're both at me, I'm skidding madly, zooming, doing flat turns, quick rolls, anything to stop them getting a bead on me, throwing the poor old Pup around, my gentle sensitive Pup, her startled shudders of protest almost hurt, but there's no smooth flying in a shambles like this, it's ham-fisted stuff or you're out.'
>
> Arthur Gould Lee

Aviation was in its infancy but little time was wasted in fitting these frail aircraft of spruce and canvas with machine guns, thus birth to a new phenomenon; aerial combat. Unlike the antiquated thinking that led to the perennial stalemate of trench warfare, aerial warfare was unprecedented and as such was unfettered by old ideas; it was created in the moment and pilots tested their ideas using their hides as collateral. If it worked; a new manoeuvre was born; if not they perished. Those who excelled at this new type of warfare gave birth to a new term; the ace.

The British Prime Minister Lloyd George stated that British pilots were the 'cavalry of the clouds' upholding a 'chivalry of the air' long abandoned by those in the trenches.[1] Adrian Smith wrote that:

> 'in a long, corrosive and morale-sapping war of attrition the public could gain some small comfort from an idealized, if in fact banal, notion that day after day brave young knights of the air took to the skies astride their mechanical chargers'[2]

Eric Leed described 'how the myth of the flier was equally powerful on the front line, reminding battle-weary and often disillusioned soldiers why they originally joined up.'[3] The mythology of the ace generated a much-needed hope that aerial warfare might eventually break the stalemate that had claimed so many lives. Interestingly, aces such as Mick Mannock 'snubbed anyone eager to lionize a glamorous fighter pilot'.[4] In contrast, German ace Ernst Udet believed 'that even in modern warfare there is still something left of the knightly chivalry of bygone days.'[5] Cecil Lewis had this to say about the mystique of the ace:

> 'Flying was still something of a miracle. We who practiced it were thought very brave, very daring, very gallant: we belonged to a world apart. In certain respects it was true, and though I do not think we traded on this adulation, we could not but be conscious of it.'[6]

National Air & Space Museum Senior Curator Dr Tom Crouch commented that even though the Second World War remains one of the most popular wars in collective memory, few non-aviation enthusiasts can remember aces from it. In strident contrast, almost everyone has heard of the Red Baron, who has come down as a kind of folk-hero.

Aces came from various backgrounds, but all showed an aptitude for aerial combat. Some were slow to learn like Raoul Lufbery of the famed *Escadrille Americane* (later the Lafayette Escadrille), whereas others such as Manfred von Richthofen, seemed to take to it instantly. Background had little to do with aptitude; however, those who were privileged had access to aircraft much sooner than those of modest means.

France, Germany and later America were quick to publicize the exploits of their star fighter pilots. Aces such as Georges Guynemer were elevated to the status of demigods thanks to the efforts of publicists such as Jacques Mortane. The German high command was quick to capitalize on their best pilots: Max Immelmann, Oswalde Boelcke, then von Richthofen and Udet. Edward V. Rickenbacker was America's Ace of Aces—a title the ace despised as:

> 'Mingled with this natural desire to become the leading fighting ace of America was a haunting superstition that did not leave my mind until the very end of the war. It was that the possession of this title – Ace of Aces – brought with it the unavoidable doom that had overtaken all its previous holders. I wanted it and yet I feared to learn that it was mine! In later days I began to feel that this superstition was the heaviest burden that I carried with me into the air. Perhaps it served to

redouble my caution and sharpened my fighting senses. But never was I able to forget that the life of a title-holder is short.'[7]

England made it policy to refrain from mentioning its pilot's exploits in the press. Or as A.G. Lee explained it:

> 'Accounts of the glorious feats of both German and French Aces received world-wide publicity, especially the United States, where the absence of similar reports on the work of British Flyers sometimes caused raised eyebrows. The precedent set by the French and Germans was followed by Belgium, Austria, Italy and in due course America. Only the British stubbornly refused to publicize their successful airman. We in the RFC could not understand the stick-in-the-mud attitude and did not realize that it was due chiefly to our own much-respected Chief, General Trenchard. In the summer of 1917, Field Marshal Haig wrote to the CIGS in London that he--which meant Trenchard-- considered it both 'unwise policy and unfair to other branches of the service to differentiate the treatment of the RFC" and that "such special treatment would be invidious and likely to cause jealousy both inside and outside the RFC".'[8]

However, due to mounting public pressure, the War Office finally allowed the press to publish articles on aces such as James McCudden, Billy Bishop, Edwin Cole and a few others. Moreover, once the 'cloak of secrecy' was lifted in 1918 Edward 'Mick' Mannock and William Barker were recognized. However, it was too little too late, as the image of the German and French Aces had in the meantime been cultivated to such burnished glory and honour that the British aces could not attain the same aura, even though their victory scores were higher.[9]

A.G. Lee concluded by stating that:

> 'What Trenchard and those who thought like in failed to realize was that human beings needed heroes, indeed pray for them, especially in wartime. The fighting troops, both in the air and on the ground, need heroes to set the standards, to lead an aggressive action, to excite imitative valour, or as General Douglas Haig wrote about Albert Ball "to act as an example and incentive" to the public who needed heroes if for no other reason, to continue support for the war and sustain morale.'[10]

AERO-NEUROSIS

British ace Captain Albert Ball rose to fame due to his expert flying, marksmanship, and tactics. He scored 44 confirmed victories at the time of his death.

Michael Paris has argued that that aviators were a 'special breed' and embodied the 'ultimate hero' and that this notion was embedded in society long before 1914.[11]

Jacques Mortanes interviewed Guynemer about his status as an ace:

> 'I asked Guynemer: As to Richthofen, I have had a project in my mind for some time. You know that they published the memoirs of Boelcke, Immelmann and Richthofen in Germany. Their aim was to exalt their Aces and to deprecate ours. It was with a view to making propaganda among the neutrals and to increase the enthusiasm for aviation among the Boches, that they were published. I believe that it would be good for the French people for you to publish your recollections. What do you say to it?
>
> '"I understand your reasoning completely," answered the Ace of Aces, "but I would never do that while the war lasts: even if the Government were to allow it, where would I find the time? Finally, even if these two conditions were met, I still would not do it, because then there would be a lot of people who would claim that I am a pretentious poseur. Let the imbeciles talk." But please consider the historic value of recounting your aerial feats for the public, and how you felt while fighting in the air. "That would be wonderful! What could I add to what you already know, for I have answered all of your questions." Yes, but that is not the same thing, Never mind all that! For your "Boche Hunters" I have pointed out two or three corrections which were not accurate; for your article in *Je Sais Tout* regarding my first thirty-six victories, my father helped you fill in the details, and therefore if you want to write about me, I shall not stop you and will furnish you with all the facts you may require, but regarding writing about myself, I will not do it.'[12]

Chapter 6

Coping with the Strain; Aviation Psychiatry

Dr Graeme Anderson found that 'nervous breakdowns have been noted since the early days of flying... aero-neurotic conditions may be brought on, firstly, simply by the strain of learning to fly.'[1] After the war began, combat compounded the problems of the aviator; what was once a collegial and competitive sport, was now an adversarial fight to the death. Furthermore, when these air fighters chose to confront their humanity, seeing their victims as fellow human beings, they suffered greatly.

Anderson coined the term 'aero-neuroses' and argued that among the terms of the day used to describe this condition it was more appropriate as it included 'any type exhibiting manifestations of functional disease of the nervous system brought on by flying.'[2] Other terms used to describe these ailments were: flying stress; flying sickness and aviators' neurasthenia; and aerosthenia. However, these terms tend to imply that the problems arose from flying specifically, or as we shall see later, the context in which the flying occurred, not by the notion of aerial combat itself or, in short the killing of fellow fliers, sometimes in a horrific way.

Addressing this subject somewhat imperfectly, Anderson stated that 'neurasthenia may follow the added strain of war-time flying with its attendant long flights, great altitudes, night flights, aerial fighting, and anti-aircraft fire.'[3] Still the subject of watching a fellow aviator go down in flames or some other horrible incident resulting from mechanized warfare was avoided, most likely due to the fact that the doctors had no way of knowing what actually occurred in the context of a dogfight.[4] Anderson did note that it would be useful for the medical profession to fly as passengers to cultivate empathy and understanding. Really what happened to these fliers was a synthesis of shell shock and flying – or mechanized warfare in the air – both were new to the human experience.

The term shell-shock was first given medical credibility by C.S. Myers in a *Lancet* paper published in February 1915. Frederick Mott was appointed by the War Office to investigate shell-shock, and he concluded that shell shock was physical in origin.[5] In other words, it was caused by concussive blasts from artillery shell detonations that damaged the brain and central nervous system. In strident contrast, Myers suggested a psychological causation and 'interpreted shellshock as a conversion disorder experienced by soldiers unable to cope with the strain of combat.'[6] The important corollary was that the military leadership begrudgingly conceded that shell-shock was psychological in origin, as it enabled casualties to return to the Front after treatment.[7] William H.R. Rivers proposed a 'psychodynamic' explanation for shell-shock, arising when 'hastily implanted defence mechanisms collapsed when faced with 'strains such as have never previously been known in the history of mankind'.'[8] This was really at the heart of both shell-shock and aero-neurosis; the dawn of full bore mechanized warfare was juxtaposed with men who simply had no (psychological) preparation for what awaited them. Since the leadership had not envisaged what would occur on the Western Front, how could those under them? After the war, Lord Home, formerly a general staff officer, commented, 'I think everyone will agree that under the novel conditions that are met with on a modern battlefield there is no man who does not suffer from fright.'[9]

Combat aviation psychiatry (and enhanced definitions of 'shell shock[10]') evolved symbiotically with the war. The diagnosis and treatment of both ground and aerial disorders was skewed towards getting the men back to the trenches or cockpits quickly. Many were regarded as cowards or 'malingerers' which tended to compound these men's difficulties, as before the war psychosis was typically thought of in terms of heredity and physiology but by 1918, many clinicians thought 'context' could be a chief factor'. Nonetheless, the traumatic event was judged secondary: 'the personality of the soldier remained the primary explanation why only some soldiers broke down in combat.'[11] Reid wrote that 'the language of cowardice permeates the wartime discourse and even in its absence doctors assumed that war neurosis arose in men who were predisposed to some kind of mental breakdown and were therefore flawed, if not culpable.'[12] Ted Bogacz wrote that after the war:

> 'There was widespread fear after the Armistice that among the 3000 soldiers convicted by courts-martial for cowardice, desertion or other crimes (of whom 346 were executed) there were a considerable number who had been suffering from war-induced mental illness and thus had been unjustly sentenced.'[13]

COPING WITH THE STRAIN; AVIATION PSYCHIATRY

Those who made these assessments were not subject to the full brunt of mechanized warfare so were falling back on old definitions of psychosis, probably from the last examples in recent memory: the Russo-Sino War; the Boer War; the Franco-Prussian War; and, further back, the Napoleonic Wars. Importantly, few had flown in an aeroplane or endured a prolonged artillery barrage, and none had flown in combat or killed another man.

Whether it was shell-shock or being physically wounded, it often resulted in a removal from duty to one of many convalescent hospitals that cropped up like mushrooms across the French and English countryside as a result of the Somme Offensive. This battle brought shell shock and neurasthenic conditions to a head, as there were thousands of shell-shock cases which compelled the army to create 'Casualty Clearing Stations' in France; there were upwards of three hundred towns in which these stations were located, often with multiple stations in each town. For example, in the towns that began with the letter 'A' there were around 61 casualty clearing stations, and 12 Hospitals (noted as 'Stationary') one of these being a BRCS or British Red Cross Society hospital. Hospitals were near the coast and were broken down into two classes: Base (or 'Stationary') and General. These were staffed by men from the Royal Army Medical Corps, Royal Engineers, and Army Service Corps.[14] The idea behind the Casualty Clearing Stations being that after a rest, the affected soldiers or pilots could be returned to duty. The French set up forward neurology centres designed to give a traumatized soldier a chance to rest and ultimately return to the trenches. Meyers co-opted this approach by recommending 'the creation of four specialist units in a position of safety but within the sound of gunfire. Called Not Yet Diagnosed Nervous (NYDN) centres, they had three core characteristics: proximity (close to the battlefield), immediacy (rapid referral from the frontline), and expectation of recovery.'[15] The problem was that the effects of combat fatigue were cumulative, not to be easily erased, much less cured, by time away. By June 1918, there were six special neurological hospitals for officers and thirteen for other ranks in England.[16]

While most military mental hospitals emphasized rest, diet, baths, drugs, electro shock, pleasant distractions (such as scenery and music), and most importantly repression of war trauma, doctors such as W.H.R. Rivers of Craiglockhart in Scotland chose a bold and different direction; facing the trauma the patient experienced quickly and directly:

> 'When in place of running away from these unpleasant thoughts he faced them boldly and allowed his mind to dwell upon them

in the day, they no longer raced through his mind at night and disturbed his sleep by terrifying dreams of warfare.'[17]

Perhaps the most significant of Rivers methods involved re-education or re-direction regarding particularly painful memories. In the instance of a soldier who had seen his comrade blown to pieces, and thus suffered horrific nightmares about what he had seen, Rivers explained to him that 'the mangled state of the body of his friend was conclusive evidence that he had been killed outright and had been spared the prolonged suffering which is too often the fate of those who sustain mortal wounds'.[18]

Rivers noted that the patient's mood improved instantly and that:

> 'He saw at once that this was an aspect of his experience upon which he could allow his thoughts to dwell. He said he would no longer attempt to banish thoughts and memories of his friend from his mind, but would think of the pain and suffering he had been spared.'[19]

Rivers' methods in many cases achieved results; the patient's suffering eased dramatically. It is unclear whether any aviators were transferred to Craiglockhart, however, Rivers' semi-psychoanalytic methods of treatment can be used to explain at least some of the case studies in the following chapters.

Combat stress among flyers or what came to be broadly termed as aero-neurosis became more common as the war progressed. The stress of combat flying combined with the imperfectly understood effects cold and high altitude flying – hypoxia – which was described by Arthur Lee as '... heaving all the time, mouth wide open, pumping in the bitingly cold air in quick, lung-flooding gasps. I even forget the cold. My heart is thumping, and I feel almost faint.'[20] The confluence of the physical discomforts of flying (hypoxia, cold, fumes) and combat fatigue resulted in many fliers being sent either home on leave, or to a convalescent hospital for a period of rest. If they suffered chronically, such as Captain Roy Brown (chapter 9), they were often taken off front line service and eventually re-assigned to a flying school. In the case of Georges Guynemer – 'unless one has given all one has given nothing' – this was not an option.

The temporary leaves gave the pilots time to be away from fighting and afforded them the chance to immerse themselves in distractions, which did not end their suffering but did in some cases distract them enough to stop

COPING WITH THE STRAIN; AVIATION PSYCHIATRY

worrying for a time. Some, like Mick Mannock, suffered a tremendous breakdown when away from the fighting as he was finally able to vent what he had repressed while at the Front. In the final analysis, when these air fighters embraced their humanity, which involved seeing their victims as fellow human beings, they suffered greatly. Joanna Bourke wrote that:

> 'The military consequences of such fits of conscience could be serious...many military and psychological commentators denied the importance of guilt, an equal number were forced to admit that such feelings sometimes precipitated war neuroses.'[21]

Each man possessed a finite amount of emotional capital and courage. Renowned English physician Charles Moran noted that 'men wear out in war-like clothes'.[22] Seemingly, the fault lines emerged almost from the very beginning of aerial warfare. Roland Garros was one of the first to score an aerial victory during the Great War and was deeply disturbed by what he had done:

> 'The chase became more and more chaotic; we were now no higher than one thousand feet; at that moment an immense flame burst from the German engine and spread instantaneously. What was curious, the plane didn't fall, but descended in an immense spiral. The spectacle was frighteningly tragic, unreal. The descent became more pronounced for 25 seconds and ended with a fall of 100 feet and a horrible crash.'[23]

Robert Wohl stated that 'Garros confessed to a family friend that the "satisfaction" and "joy" he felt at having "created alone, and in spite of all the risks of the unknown in aviation, the instrument that brought me success."'[24] This statement did not sit well with Garros, so that he felt compelled to both explain and apologize to another friend for what Wohl describes as an 'enthusiastic and breezy account' of his first victory. Garros in a more sober and reflective mood wrote the following about the encounter:

> 'I recounted in a humorous vein my first successful combat: the thing was instead tragic and scarcely lent itself to jokes. It was horrible and I remained traumatized for some time. It was in this period of numbness that I wrote you nonsense in bad taste in order to react against my own mood.'[25]

AERO-NEUROSIS

Humour was something that was used as a coping mechanism to disguise emotional trauma among flyers. Mick Mannock used this frequently to disguise what he was feeling, as did Elliott Springs and others. Another early ace who showed signs of the strain of air fighting was Oswald Boelcke. Germany's top ace after Immelmann was killed, Boelcke began his flying as a physically fit and exuberant flyer; by the time of his death photos of one of Germany's top aces show a worried expression, with sunken eyes, and a troubled brow. One can only speculate what would have happened to him had he survived longer than he did.

Remarque commented in *All Quiet on the Western Front* on the nature of the First World War:

> 'A hospital alone shows what war is….I am 20 years old; yet I know nothing of life but to spare, death, fear, and fatuous superficiality cast over an abyss of Sorrow. I see how peoples are set against one another, and in silence, unknowingly, foolish League, obediently, innocently slay one another. I see the keenest brains of the world invent weapons and words to make it yet more refined and enduring.'[26]

Remarque continued by writing that:

> 'The first bomb, the first explosion, burst in our hearts. We are cut off from activity, from striving, from progress We believe in such things no longer, we believe in the war.'[27]

Elliott Springs writing as the character of his dead friend 'Mac' Grider felt the same way, as he described being made a 'serious man', old before his time, and only interested in the next patrol due to his war experience.[28]

This sentiment is echoed repeatedly in the writings of the pilots featured in this book, the notion that due to their transformation during their war experience they became creatures born of, and belonging to, the Great War. Importantly this transformation was final and irrevocable. Pat Barker described it as analogous to the transformation from caterpillar to butterfly: 'the process of transformation consists almost entirely of decay…what you will never find is that mythical creature, half caterpillar, half butterfly.'[29] These men were now creatures for which civilian life no longer held any appeal. The combat flying at the Front was the only thing that appealed to them even though ironically and tragically, they knew it was destroying them.

COPING WITH THE STRAIN; AVIATION PSYCHIATRY

Edwin Parsons, years after his combat experience, wrote the now classic book *I Flew with the Lafayette Escadrille*. This book contains a wealth of information and colourful reminisces, as well as frank discussions about the reality of combat flying. Parsons had this to say about the strain of combat flying:

> 'No matter whether a man is visibly scared or not by a shower of flying lead, each time it happens to him it leaves an invisible scar. He begins flinching before he know it, And in the end, the strain cuts into his nerves. If he hasn't a sedative for those strained nerves, and sometimes despite it, a bird is likely to get so screwy that he goes wild and begs for danger like dope or gets the wind up and comes completely unstuck.
>
> 'Underneath, he may have all the courage and fortitude in the world, but when his imagination gets the better of him or the constant strain is too severe and his nerves go back on him, he's no more good. It's somewhat the same as shell shock. It always leaves a scar on the nervous system, and some men have killed themselves long after the war on account of it. That's where liquor came in—to ward off those searing scars and prevent a nerve-racked buzzard from blowing up altogether...When a man heard bullets whistle by his head the first time, he was either scared pink or else he had no idea what that peculiar sound could be. Speaking for myself, there isn't any question. I was petrified, although I didn't realize to what extent till I set my wheels down on the home tarmac after the scrap and attempted to hop nonchalantly out of the ship. My knees absolutely refused to support me. They gave way like two pieces of string. And I had to wrap a shaking arm around a strut and hang on for dear life for over a minute...my head mechanic...thought I had been shot through the body at least a dozen times, My face was a greenish-yellow, and my wildly staring eyes strained through the two smudged circles which resembled burned holes in a blanket. There was a complete vacuum where my stomach should have been, and my mouth was full of heart or Adam's apple or something.'[30]

Parsons' tract touches on a number of very salient points, the notion of imagination, suicide and use of alcohol. The statement by

AERO-NEUROSIS

Dr Graeme Anderson that 'those with little or no imagination make the better fighting pilots' rings true relative to Parsons' passage. The resorting to suicide as a result of delayed trauma after the war certainly could be applied to Ernst Udet; and alcohol as a structural and necessary coping mechanism for the strain of combat flying is mentioned by many other pilots as well. Parsons' very candid account went so far as to say that judicious use of alcohol acted as 'a soporific for the agony of tortured nerves,' and continued that 'The boys whose records showed the most battles and the most official Huns were the same whose records revealed a lot of hours at the bar.'[31]

Cecil Lewis explained why he thought pilots crack up:

> 'There are times in life when the faculties seem to be keyed up to superhuman tension. You are not necessarily doing anything; but you are in a state of awareness, of tremendous alertness, ready to act instantaneously should the need arise. Outwardly, that day, I was calm, busy keeping the trenches in the camera sight, manipulating the handle, pulling the string; waiting for something, I did not know what, to happen. It was my first job. I was under fire for the first time. Would Archie get the range? Would the dreaded Fokker appear? Would the engine give out? It was the fear of the unforeseen, the inescapable, the imminent hand of death which might, from moment to moment, be ruthlessly laid upon me. I realized, not then, but later, why pilots cracked up, why they lost their nerve and had to go home. Nobody could stand the strain indefinitely, ultimately it reduced you to a dithering state, near to imbecility. For always you had to fight it down, you had to go out and do the job, you could never admit it, never say frankly: "I am afraid. I can't face it anymore." For cowardice, because, I suppose, it is the most common human emotion, is the most despised. And you did gain victories over yourself. You won and won and won again, and always there was another to be won on the morrow. They sent you home to rest, and you put it in the background of your mind; but it was not like a bodily fatigue from which you could completely recover, it was a sort of damage to the essential tissue of your being. You might have a greater will-power, greater stamina to fight down your failing; but a thoroughbred that has been lashed will rear at the sight of the whip, and never, once you had been through it, could you be quite the same again.'[32]

COPING WITH THE STRAIN; AVIATION PSYCHIATRY

Arthur Lee Gould stated that:

> 'The stock of courage which a man possesses is expendable, and he loses a little of it every time he runs a razor's edge risk. The strain is deepened if his weapon is inferior and he knows he is at a disadvantage...'[33]

As the war progressed, hospitals specifically for flyers began to emerge and one of these – Number 24 RAF General Hospital – is mentioned by Roy Brown:

> 'It is on a hill close to Hampstead Heath...They do a lot of research work here into the different kinds of troubles which are peculiar to flying people. It is purely for RAF officers so they get lots of material to work on. It is a very good idea having a hospital like this as in an ordinary hospital they do not know how to treat the troubles of flying people.'[34]

Dr H. Graeme Anderson was stationed at this hospital and wrote *The Medical and Surgical Aspects of Aviation* in 1919; undoubtedly Brown was one of his patients. Anderson's tract argued that 'those with marked powers of imagination may make the more skilful pilots as far as actually handling a machine goes, but those with little or no imagination make the better fighting pilots' which rings true, and he continued: 'to send a patient away on sick leave who complains of sleeplessness, headaches, nightmares, and shows signs of general nervous instability without any further word or examination, is to condemn him to a great deal of mental and physical suffering', which resonates with the men described in this book. The US government published the *Air Medical Manual* in 1918 but this tract focused on physiological aspects of flying such as proper nutrition and temperament and does not delve into psychological matters at all.

Many (such as Roy Brown) were discharged from hospital to serve in a reduced capacity as flight instructors. Some were granted a series of leaves as bureaucrats and military and medical leadership struggled with what to do with these men. Publication of this type of trauma was considered counterproductive to the war effort so treatment and diagnosis tended to amplify the effects of high altitude flying and various physiological disorders, such as *Air Medical*, and downplayed the psychological trauma experienced by combat flyers. It was no coincidence that Anderson's tract

AERO-NEUROSIS

was published after the war. In addition, *Notes on Practical Flying* was published in 1918 and is written for flight training, not combat. This tract describes common sense methods and scenarios which were the antithesis of that which occurred during the war. The following is a passage describing proper physiological conditions under which the student should fly and an almost monolithic denial of any psychological issues that were manifest:

> 'Alcohol is better avoided altogether, and, similarly, excess in smoking, which may cause palpitation, faintness and double vision. Most aviators smoke too much. Diet should be generous and nourishing, as there is a good deal of nerve strain and wear and tear of the nervous system during this period. Flying when hungry is to be avoided, as faintness may occur in the air. Proper sleep is most important, and 8 hours sound sleep in the 24 hours should be obtained. Well-regulated physical training is of great value, and pupils should be afforded every recreation of mind and body at an air station. With regard to the psychology of flying, or the study of the sensations in the air, it has been found from an analysis of 100 confessions of pupils after their first solo flights that the mind is so occupied in paying attention to flying, watching instruments, controls, etc., that fear has rarely time to assert itself, at least, not enough to disturb their flying.'[35]

Now compare this last statement to the one by Dr Anderson, who actually spent time in a war hospital: 'aero-neurotic conditions may be brought on, firstly, simply by the strain of learning to fly.' Obviously, the *Notes on Practical Flying* would be more accurately titled *Notes on Flight Training* as this is precisely what it describes, but even this does not square Anderson's statement with those in the tract. Importantly, this tract was written in the context of the US government attempting to simultaneously build, train, and deploy an air force, while concurrently trying to codify this new field for itself; it is more idealized and aspirational than practical.

Of the case studies included in the following chapters, each fits rather imperfectly into the following psychological categories: contrition, repression, and sublimation; most were combinations of all three. Those who confronted their fears openly and honestly suffered the least – Ernst Udet for example. Those who repressed their anxieties suffered an emotional collapse, such as William Lambert. Most were hybrids of all

COPING WITH THE STRAIN; AVIATION PSYCHIATRY

three qualities. For example, Mick Mannock was able to sublimate his fears into a constructive purpose, yet suffered in the privacy of his quarters or when among close friends.

All of the medical manuals that came out at the conclusion of the war agree on at least one point: that an imagination is not desirable for a combat flyer. Yet, this was a war fuelled by the imagination; horrific weapons born from the recesses of perverted science coalescing in a context that was stationary (trench warfare). Each new machine, be they aeroplanes, tanks, zeppelins, epic artillery, were clearly in the realm of the fantastic giving credence to movements such as 'futurism' or modernism in the arts. How can the average human being insulate himself or deny such fantastic sights and experiences?

Ben Shephard wrote in *A War of Nerves*: 'We hear more from doctors than from patients. However hard he tries, the historian cannot even the account, cannot give the patients an equal voice, because most of them chose not to recount their experiences.'[36] Some pilots' letters were fortunately published after 1919 which contain a wealth of material that elucidates what they were experiencing. For those who could not put their suffering into words, their friends sometimes did.

Chapter 7

Elliott White Springs – the True War Bird

'Fear will cause you to die' so men must 'get angry and kill' wrote Marine instructor Captain Wilfred T. Colyner; this sentiment could be applied to many combat aviators including Elliott W. Springs.[1]

Leroy Springs was a textile industrialist in Lancaster, South Carolina. As his entrepreneurial success increased, he married Grace Allison White of Fort Mill in 1891. Elliot White Springs was born in 1896. Grace died in 1907 at 33 when Elliot was 10. Elliott's maternal grandmother died four years earlier; the shock of this was especially pronounced for Elliott as he found her body. In 1908 Leroy sent Elliott to Asheville School in NC where Elliott had no family support. While here he began a toxic correspondence with Leroy who urged him to do better in his schoolwork and to avoid sports that might cause physical harm. Even at this early age Elliott recognized and resisted the strong and insistent will of his father. In response, Elliott developed methods of deflecting his father's will that continued until Leroy's death in 1931.[2]

After completing school in Asheville, Leroy decided to send Elliott to Culver Military Academy in Indiana from 1911-1913, where he developed an interest in writing stories, withdrawing further into his imagination to compensate for the lack of a normal family life. Leroy married his second wife, Lena, in 1913. Lena was a mover and a shaker and Elliott never completely accepted her as a substitute for his mother; Lena was unconcerned.[3]

Elliott attended Princeton University where he focused on literature classes, his professors including E.C. McDonald and Alfred Noyes, yet he was unable to convince either of them that he would make a good writer. Classmates included F. Scott Fitzgerald and John Peale Bishop who Springs must have known although they did not become friends.[4] When war erupted in 1914, Elliott felt the call; he wanted to be an aviator.

ELLIOTT WHITE SPRINGS – THE TRUE WAR BIRD

The relationship between Elliott, Leroy and Lena comprised almost entirely of letters written to each other as Elliott travelled from place to place and continued during his war years. Given this context, one can easily see how important the letters would become to anyone as they constituted the sum of exchanges between father, son and stepmother. Among many things stressed by Springs was his desire to keep his letters about his wartime activities private. He found sharing of such wartime experiences by others in the press most distasteful:

> 'Dear Father---I hear that you passed on one of my letters to Mr. Brewster and he passed it around generally. The last thing I asked you before I left was please not to pass my letters around. I also *wrote you* asking you not to pass them around.'
> (4 Dec 1917 from Stamford, Lincolnshire)[5]

This could also explain the serial frustration that both men experienced when the letters did not contain enough heartfelt sentiment or details; letters are a poor substitute for actually growing up with one's parents under the same roof. Springs writes of his dissatisfaction with the content of both his father's and stepmother's letters repeatedly:

> 'Dear Mother – To say that I am furious is putting it very mildly. In the first place you needn't write at all. This is my last effort. You all must care a lot about me at home. Not enough to write to me anyway, and you haven't enough pride to take any trouble to write a decent letter. In the second place…Father had been showing those pictures I sent you to everyone in the state who was polite enough to look at them. I boil, I seethe, I spit fire.'
> (6 Feb 1918, London Colney, Hertfordshire, 56 Training sq.)[6]

The motivation for such exaggerated frustrations is simple; a son who never got a proper childhood or a nurturing home life growing up. Letters from Leroy contain advice, requests for detailed information and cautions to Elliott to be careful. Elliott's responses to his father's letters were sometimes informative, other times downright nasty and caustic. However, they always closed with 'a heartful of love'. The lack of a normal home life could also explain Springs' close bond with those with whom he fought, especially John 'Mac' Grider and Larry Callahan; the 'Three Musketeers'. John MacGavock Grider, was born on 28 May 1892 at Sans Souci. He married Marguerite Samuels in the

AERO-NEUROSIS

fall of 1909 and they had two sons. A few years later he separated from his wife and returned to the huge Sans Souci plantation where he was farming when the US declared war on Germany, resulting in his enlistment. When Grider died in June 1918 it hit Springs very hard. Springs refered repeatedly in his letters to missing Grider and wishing he could still be with him and Callahan.

Springs was trained at London Colney presumably on Sopwith Pups and Spads as his flight log lists both of these planes. I believe he was having difficulty with the Spad, as the Pup is a very docile aeroplane to fly: 'I've gotten 8 hours in three days – on a new machine – most difficult thing made to fly – and it keeps me in a cold sweat all the time.'[7] This passage could suggest early neurasthenia, however; learning to fly a new aircraft during this period was undoubtedly stressful.

William 'Billy' Bishop had been given authority to hand pick men for his squadron, 85. He met Grider, Springs, and Callahan (25 or 26 March 1918) and decided he wanted them in his squadron. Bishop got a confirmation on 1 April to make this so. The 'Three Musketeers' were transferred to the military flying field at Hounslow to join 85 Squadron,[8] which was equipped with the S.E.5a. On June 18, Bishop was withdrawn from service due to fears that he would be killed in combat or taken prisoner. Bishop was furious; both the British and Canadian governments felt that he was more valuable as an inspirational leader than as a fighter pilot. Mannock replaced Bishop on 21 June. [9]

Springs' baptism of fire shook him up as evidenced by his reaction to a particularly bad 'Archie' or anti-aircraft barrage:

> 'Then a new chapter in my life began. I am now a changed man. I got sensations I never knew existed before. About three Hun batteries appeared just in front of me and I swung around just in time to avoid it. Scared – of course I was scared – scared stiff. Heavy clouds below. [he describes getting pounded and becoming disoriented in a field of flak—finally he makes a run for it] ...after an age, he [the flak battery] stopped [firing], so I caught my breath and wondered how to get home, as it was getting dark.'[10]

A short time later he had become numb to Archie so that he made the following comment in one of his letters: 'My nerves are in excellent condition due to regular doses of Archie and I have long since quit biting my nails.'[11]

ELLIOTT WHITE SPRINGS – THE TRUE WAR BIRD

Apparently, life in a British squadron agreed with Springs. The following commentary on what he perceived as a cultural tendency is illuminating and caught Springs off-guard such that he found it difficult to express what he was feeling. The expression of feelings that was considered 'extremely bad form' was argued by Rivers as working against psychological health:

> 'Everyone thinks of the English as having a phlegmatic disposition. Nothing could be further from the truth. It is considered extremely bad form to display the slightest emotion. An Englishman will get news of the death of his brother, son, or father, or the elopement of his wife, be awarded the V.C. or lose a leg and merely raise an eyebrow. And ten minutes later sit down to dinner and show no trace of emotion. But they feel anything more than any other race…no rotten sentimentality about it and yet you'd be surprised how deeply these Englishmen feel things and how much sentimentality they have in their nature. I can't do justice to the subject so will cease.'[12]

Springs was quick to perceive the war as a personal attack on him alone. This arrogance is characteristic of the man, and he was also quick to seek revenge—patiently and in a calculating fashion:

> 'You'd be surprised how personal the war in the air gets. Whenever there's anything doing you always know that each little lead pellet or Archie shell was meant for you personally. And when you fire you don't just fire towards Berlin and hope that some Hun stops it. Nope, you wait till you see a special particular Hun, you may wait three or four days for him, and then you let fly.'[13] [June 1918]

In Springs' diary entry of 18 June, he records:

> 'Mac and I doing high protection spot a Rumpler near Menin. We get it. Mac Missing. Oh Christ. Am I to blame.'[14]

He was clearly shocked at the loss of his friend and instantly wondered if it was his fault; he still held out hope that Mac would turn up however, and apparently was chastised for losing Grider from the flight by commander Captain Horn.[15] Springs recounted the last time he saw Grider on the fateful patrol of 18 June:

> 'Mac Grider is no longer with us. I started back for where the lines were, steering by the sun. I looked back and Mac was following. After five or ten minutes I got my bearings and got back to the patrol. But that's the last I've seen of him.'[16]
>
> 'No man ever had a truer friend and the fact that we fought together and in unison and harmony shows the confidence we had in one another. And he was as fine a fighter as ever tripped a trigger.'

Springs refused to give up hope that he might still be alive although he wrestled with the notion, as time elapsed, that he was gone forever. In writing to his stepmother his anguish and frustration over the loss of his friend took the form of refreshed anger at Lena, perhaps that a true friend was gone and she was a poor substitute:

> 'Mac is gone but he'll never be forgotten until the Hun's aim improves or my bus goes back on me – or I pass out from irritation at the doings of the Springs family on the home front…anyway, I hope my ghost haunts you and never gives you a moment's peace…I could sleep with great ease right now…but instead I'm writing to you until time to go up on patrol at seven and try to avenge Mac. May your powdered nose take on the colour of an overripe tomato and my you never see your feet again except in a mirror! I'm completely fed up with you.'[17] [18 June 1918, St. Omer France]

Most First World War aviators did not enjoy strafing enemy troops, with perhaps the notable exception of von Richthofen. Springs clearly didn't like it:

> '…If you know you're going around straffing [sic] the next day you don't sleep as well as you might. That's the job we all hate. I'll write you about it sometime but its not a pleasant subject.'[18]

Strafing of troops and fighters armed with bombs marked the beginning of tactical air support for ground troops.

ELLIOTT WHITE SPRINGS – THE TRUE WAR BIRD

On 27 June 1918 he crashed his S.E.5a in Nieppe forest. He suffered severe lacerations to his head due to impacting the machine gun mount. He was taken to the Duchess of Sutherland Hospital, where he wrote the following letter to his mother:

> 'Dear Mother – Well, I'm a casualty – that's what comes of playing with these Huns – they have no sense of humor… when I arrived I was full of anti-tetanus serum, morphine, and brandy – unusually full. Naturally I acted a bit queer and now the doc is convinced that I am suffering with acute concussion… but who wouldn't act crazy with that combination? And who wouldn't rave after they'd gone twenty miles over after a Hun, gotten him and then have both guns jam and then get shot up yourself…the whole Hun army shooting at you all the way… wouldn't you rave?'[19]

Seemingly, Springs was delirious and in a semi-hysterical state which is understandable, although he obviously sought empathy or at least sympathy from his stepmother. He continued to explain his erratic behaviour as:

> '…you can't expect me to enthuse over an entirely new face that resembles nothing I've ever seen before… they brought my machine back in six lumps…but my face – oh, mother, it's awful. They'll use me after the war as propaganda – the horrors of warfare.'[20]

From the hospital he wrote to Leroy telling him of his transfer in late June of 1918:

> '..I've been promoted and I don't know what to do about it. A telegram came through for me to report to another squadron yesterday as a flight commander [148th Aero]. I suppose that'll mean a captaincy in time, say three or four months. But I don't want it.'[21]

Both the 148th and 17th Aero were fully manned by Americans, including maintenance personnel – the British supplied the aircraft and assigned them their missions. Their task was to support the BEF not the AEF. They were flying Sopwith Camels, which by mid-summer 1918 were becoming obsolete, especially against the Fokker D. VII.[22] The new commanding officer of 148th, Captain Morton 'Mort' Newhall, transferred from 84 squadron and the unit moved to Capelle, three miles south of Dunkirk. On 2 July, Springs arrived and was assigned commander of B flight. He suffered a relapse[23] resulting in his absence from 8-28 July. The Squadron became operational on the 20th.[24] Regarding his physical condition, Springs wrote:

> 'My hands, feet, and joints swelled double their size, my eyes closed completely – the remnants of my lips doubled up, my tongue broke out, my face looked like a big lump of red putty. I itched all over, my stomach broke out on the inside and wouldn't receive even water – I ached all over – my head split. The doctor replied "you must have been the baby at home."'[25]

Joanna Bourke wrote that 'although the medical officer must show sympathy, the patient must be induced to face his illness in a manly way',[26] which could explain the doctor's sarcastic comment regarding Springs injuries. Medical staff recommended that Springs take leave in England for 7-10 days, but Springs was somewhat recalcitrant as he wanted to get back in the fight.[27] The doctors explained to him that the crash produced a slight haemorrhage of the retina in the back of his eyes, which would ultimately cure itself. Springs finally conceded to take leave in Paris.[28] In a letter to his stepmother on 27 July, he wrote 'Well I am an old man. The mirror shows no white hairs but mental reflection shows unmistakable signs of old age.'[29] He made the following humorous comment about the shortage of sugar:

> 'The Paris charmers will laugh at jewelry, scorn frat pins, bread tickets and Hun souvenirs, but just mention the fact that you have some sugar, well it's like getting careless with a limousine at the Frolics.'[30]

The next day he returned to the squadron.

In spite of his injuries and the dangers of aerial combats, Springs tried to keep the tone of his letters upbeat, which his father interpreted as 'frivolities'. The lag time in correspondence often fuelled the frustration over their exchanges, as, by the time a letter reached home, the response was drafted, and sent back, it could take weeks to reach Springs. The following is typical of the types of letters Springs received from Leroy:

ELLIOTT WHITE SPRINGS – THE TRUE WAR BIRD

'Now my dear son, I do not think it fair to treat us this way. You should have cabled us when you were hurt and your letter is so unsatisfactory to us. You do not state how you were hurt, what the accident consisted of, whether you were shot down in your machine, or how it happened. I am very much worried but thankful that you are out again. Please sit down and write us full particulars and do not deal in frivolities...'[31]

The official squadron history describes Springs as being:

'a fine pilot and flight-leader but more impetuous, more willing to take chances, the last to leave a fight and the first to commence one. He would never desert a pilot in distress, several times he nearly lost his life vainly trying to save a pilot, who was hopelessly fighting against odds.'[32]

He was not going to let another one get away after Mac, whom he felt he had abandoned. Springs wanted Larry Callahan in the 148th to reunite the two remaining 'Musketeers' so Callahan transferred from the 85th in early September 1918, serving as assistant B flight commander, and replaced Springs in October as B flight commander. Springs developed a no-nonsense attitude toward combat flying, combining what he learned from Bishop and Mannock:

'It is foolish to fight EA [enemy aircraft] scouts except when it is possible to start the fight from above. If above and there are no other machines in sight, dive, fire at close range only and then pull up in a climbing turn and go down again. This avoids a dog fight and makes it possible to break off the fight [if other EA approach]. If below enemy scouts, as soon as they are seen, turn back to our lines and climb into the sun. When above the enemy machines come down from the sun as before...If you cannot attack with the advantage, don't attack.'[33]

Regarding the Sopwith Camel, Springs flew these against the vastly superior Fokker D. VII. The following is his opinion regarding the tactics necessary in fighting the Fokkers with the Camel:

'A tricky little biplane [the Camel] ... they would do about 90 mph level but you couldn't fly level because they would

AERO-NEUROSIS

shake your teeth out in forty seconds by the clock. You had to climb or glide. But they could fly upside down and turn inside a stairwell. They would stall at 15,000 feet and lose 1,000 in a turn. But they were deadly below 5,000 feet if you could suck the Fokkers down to that level.'[34]

148th squadron obtained rebuilt Camels from Aire, as no new ones had been built since January 1918 when they became obsolete, and were replaced by S.E.5as, Dolphins, Bentleys, and Snipes. But during the summer of 1918 they were still the workhorses below 15,000 feet according to Springs.[35] Springs continued by stating that:

'the Camel [was at a] disadvantage…where speed and height were paramount, but in a dogfight down low nothing could get away from it… a Camel could make a monkey out of an SE or a Fokker at treetop level but it couldn't zoom and it couldn't dive. The Dolphin was worthless because the motors were too unreliable and the Bentleys and Snipes didn't get to the front until too late.'[36]

As late as 30 July, Springs noted that there was still no news of Mac Grider, and on his birthday – 31 July – he wrote that he never expected to last this long and make it to 22 years old. At this time, he also received the official word that Grider had been killed in action.[37] Springs did not have much time to allow this sobering piece of news sink in, as on 8 August, the combined allied forces launched the 100 days offensive; attacking all along the Western Front. General Ludendorff called it a 'black day' for the German army, a turning point in war after which the Germans were forever on the defensive.[38] During the period between 8 August and 29 September, Springs participated in some of the most stressful flying of the war, which was exacerbated by his concern for other pilots in his flight. As fewer pilots returned safely, he became more anxious about his own odds. His letters home remained cheerful; however, when examining his flight logs the stresses and strains are more obvious.[39] Duties at this time comprised bomber escort, strafing, and dropping small bombs. This is characteristic of late war flying when mobility had at last replaced the stasis of trench warfare and aircraft now worked closely with the infantry in coordinated tactical air support roles.

David Vaughan wrote that during this period (just under two months) what is surprising is not that Springs and others suffered physical and emotional breakdowns during and after the war, but that they did not suffer it sooner and more completely. Henry Clay commander of C flight writing home confided: 'latter part of September, my nerves were pretty near gone.'[40]

Springs experienced his most difficult and challenging aerial combats from the airfield at Remaisnil; during this period a film crew wanted to shoot footage of the squadron for propaganda purposes. Springs sarcastically gave them a screenplay for front line air fighting:

> 'Our fearless airmen "leaping into the air" then "take off". Then insert "two hours later" and show the planes returning all shot up. All return but one. Then show a close-up of the C.O. shading his eyes and scanning the skies nervously. But the last plane returns not. Then show the mechanics stroking the lost pilot's hat and shoes tearfully. Show the flight commander tearfully explaining how he was saved by having a Fokker shot off his tail by an act of sacrifice. Let them summon the chaplain and hold prayers and then summon the YMCA secretary and have a song service. Then have the multitude break into triumphant shouts as the long lost plane is sighted, staggering home under its load of lead and just at that moment the general arrives with sackful of medals. Get six French women and dress them up as German mothers and have them weep profusely. Then dress them up as American mothers and show them grinning joyously holding up six Iron Crosses. And finish it up with a close-up of the President.'[41]

By 14 August, in a letter to his stepmother, Springs was having nightmares about his combats with Fokker D. VIIs:

> 'Dear Mother, I'm not feeling well today. I fought Huns in my sleep and after two hours more today I feel all washed out. Yesterday produced the worst scrap that I shall ever have the opportunity to indulge in. It lasted about twenty minutes and the participants were nine new type Hun Scouts [Fokker D. VII] and myself...each Hun fired at me at least once and I fired at each one [once] then several times collectively and individually.'[42]

AERO-NEUROSIS

Eddie Rickenbacker also noted that:

> '...It is a thrilling and a somewhat fearful sight to see the outline of a Fokker biplane descending upon one. I see them in my dreams very frequently after too hearty a supper late at night.'[43]

Springs wanted his family to have some record of his time in France which is why he included such vivid details of his combats. He wrote each time as if it might be his last:

> '...I feel if I get away with anything over here you and Father have a right to know about it. And as something may happen to me at any time I feel I ought to write to you about it. But that is all. No one else is to know about it or have an opportunity to use their imagination...I know several who have done well over here and have their pictures in all the papers at home and I feel sorry for them. It's not their fault either. Thank goodness I'm working with the British where such rot isn't countenanced. But my nerves are a bit touchy today...I certainly miss Mac Grider.'[44]

Springs was carrying the weight of Mac's loss which was compounded by the strain of late war fighting; the Germans fought with a ferocity born of desperation. His flight log for 15 and 16 August noted that he was attacked by 4 and 5 Fokkers respectively. He wrote that the fight on the 16th was 'the worst dogfight you ever saw. Everybody shooting at everybody else. 20 Huns and 11 of us.'[45] Springs again notes what excellent aircraft the Fokker D.VIIs were but that the pilots were 'dud',[46] most likely due to the fact that, in its desperation, Germany was rushing green pilots into the cockpits of the D. VIIs which were designed to be easy to fly; not necessarily easy to fly well. Springs showed a particular disdain or sarcasm for United States' war efforts – America had not had a war on her native soil since the Civil War; wars abroad must have seemed a curiosity to some:

> 'Picked up some souvenirs for you all while I was at the front. The American Army claims to be fighting for democracy, but the British and French say we are fighting for souvenirs. And the doughboys say they are fighting to make the world safe for prohibition.'[47]

ELLIOTT WHITE SPRINGS – THE TRUE WAR BIRD

Springs sensed he was not going to make it home alive; it came down to a choice between getting killed or cracking up, and a profound appreciation of life:

> '...I don't know which is going to get me first, a bullet or nervous strain. Playing bait is the most desperate game in the world and unless properly played is the most deadly. That's all I've been doing for the past two weeks and its beginning to tell. I'll never be able to shoot at a bird. I know too well how it feels.'[48]

Near the end of August, Springs wrote to his stepmother about his new found fatalism which was common among many First World War flyers—a liminal zone between nervous exhaustion and the desire to die and end the war with honour:

> 'Again I've got that feeling, gee, it's great to be alive. The last three days have been particularly strenuous and eventful. Ordinarily I wouldn't be able to sleep at all but I'm getting so hardened to it that I slept like a baby last night. And I'm getting so bored at being shot at that I don't bother to dodge anymore. I sat in the midst of Archie bursts yesterday for five minutes and yawned, refused to turn until they knocked me about thirty feet.'[49]

James Norman Hall escaped the carnage of western civilization by moving to Tahiti after the war – the following statement indicates that perhaps others discussed this as well:

> 'The next [thing you know] you are so fed up you want to go to a South Sea Isle where they don't know whether war is a vegetable or a new kind of barbed wire.'[50]

Springs recorded a vivid description of a duel with a Fokker D. VII and the important difference between air and ground fighting:

> 'whether you win or lose is immaterial – you see it through and rejoice then and for a day or so after. The smell of powder up in the air has an effect indescribable. But the waiting around, the hot air, red tape, and pettiness on the ground disgusts you.

> While you are in the air you are so far above the smallness of [human?] nature and stupidity that the contrast on the ground is disgusting…but when you're ordered up to go ground strafing or go for balloons you feel that the man who gives the order is nothing more or less than an executioner and if he makes you wait around all day he's nothing more or less than an accomplished torturer.'[51]

Springs felt frustrated that the US was publicizing efforts of the army air force training camps in Texas and the newly formed naval aviation unit which prompted more snide comments such as 'How's the Battle on the Texas front? Isn't it a shame the dear boys can't get over, no matter how hard they try? How are the Naval Aviators getting along? It must be awful guarding New York Harbor.' He justifies his comments by contrasting it to his own experience: 'you haven't seen real men going west every day like I have. Real men, that love fighting.'[52] Springs was also beginning to realize the human cost of their effort. The following is a reminiscence of one of his squadron mates, a man who had many noble attributes and whose death seemed meaningless:

> 'Kent Curtis was shot down by one of the Huns. A fine fellow he was, possessed of an excellent sense of humor, once a teacher of French and German at a Missouri college, once a guide in the northern woods, and a gentleman above reproach. His witty remarks will long ring in my ears, and he was a musician with few equals.'[53]

Among Springs' many worthwhile observations, perhaps one of the most insightful, was his commentary on the nerve required in air combat, and the difference between 'nerve' and 'nerves':

> 'But Lord, how this business is getting to me. Last night the old restlessness overtook me and no sleep could I get. It's not your nerve that's affected but nerves. It's your stamina, your power of endurance, that's hit by this game. A man comes out here with no nerve or nerves, and as he is just born in a man, it ain't. Recklessness, foolhardiness, fearlessness, yes, but nerve, no. Nerve is cultivated and may or may not include recklessness. It is the ability to carry through anything anywhere without

faltering. A man who rushes into a fight and then lets his hand shake on the trigger hasn't got it. And the fool who doesn't know when to be afraid hasn't got it. He'll get scared some day and spill the beans. But a man with nerve is a hardened, tempered individual who may be scared to death, but fear to him is like water on a duck's back.'[54]

Springs' flight log of 27 August states his flight was engaged with 15-20 Fokkers and that he shot one down.[55] He mentioned that there were more, but another flight got to them first. He also noted the tenacity and aggressiveness of von Richthofen's Jasta 11:

'These Huns are getting entirely too ambitious. They're almost getting offensive! Before long one of them will actually come up to the lines! ... it was the same bunch that got Tipton, Hamilton, Campbell, Williams...its von Richthofen's Old Circus and have entirely the wrong idea about this war...you can always tell them by their orange and red fuselages.'[56]

Springs writes that Bishop was too cautious, Mannock was too reckless, advocating for his own leadership as:

'trying to steer the middle course. I want to get Huns, and I try to do my work, but at the same time I'm trying to go easy on the lives of the men who are depending on me to pull them through.'[57]

He also requested at this time that Larry Callahan be transferred to his flight as he thought 'it ought to help a lot as my nerves are worn to a frazzle leading all these patrols and I can trust Larry to take a lot of work off my shoulders.'[58] On 30 August, he wrote to Leroy and mentioned that Callahan was indeed being transferred:

'Larry Callahan is coming to my flight next week and then I may be able to lay off for a week. I need a little rest. My nerves are in rotten shape and my eyes are going back on me again. Don't laugh when I say "nerves" It's no joke. Long patrols and ground strafing will get any man any time.'[59]

AERO-NEUROSIS

Springs wanted to shoot down the enemy but paradoxically he did not want the accolades, least of all the title of 'ace:'

> 'And if anybody write me again that "doubtless you hope to be an ace" I'll send them an infernal machine. I am not an "ace" don't want to be an "ace" and never will be an "ace". We don't have "aces" here. This "ace" stuff makes me tired. Call it off, wash it out! Also this individual effort stuff is all wrong. If I get any more Huns than [the other] men in my flight it's because I'm a better shot. If they don't get Huns it's because I'm a bad leader as much as anything else. My job is not to get Huns myself, but to lead my flight to the detriment of the Hun.'[60]

It is evident that Springs had adopted the collectivist attitude towards air fighting as espoused so well by Mick Mannock. However, the losses still mounted with more heated engagements with the Fokker D. VIIs. He notes on 2 September that pilots Forster, Kenyon, Frobisher, and Mandel went missing.[61] At this time he was engaged in a particularly tough dog fight with the D. VIIs such that his wing buckled and his Camel began to spin; he thought he was 'cold meat' and at that moment thought how glad Mac would be to see him.[62] He managed to land safely, and has such affection for his plane that he went to great lengths to repair it rather than taking a new Camel: 'I've got my old bus all fixed up with new wings, new tail, new engine, and new guns and am so fond of it I'm going to keep it instead of taking one of the new ones.'[63] This was common among First World War pilots. William Lambert wrote how much affection he had for his S.E.5a and was sad to part with it.

During all of Springs' increasingly stressful flying, there was one common thread; the toxic exchange of letters between his parents and himself. Springs expressed consistent dissatisfaction with the letters he received from his parents and was equally infuriated if they shared them. Springs continued to try to impress his father with his achievements although he was quick to smite any attempt Leroy made at understanding what he was experiencing; how could anyone who wasn't there? He wrote to Leroy that 'If I'm not shot down in the next six weeks I'll pull off something that you can really talk about.'[64] The following summarizes how Springs felt about his accomplishments in France:

> 'If it were the lower classes who indulged in the poor rotten cheap sentimentality, that even the French peasant scorn,

I could understand it. But no, in America our best people have proved the contention of democracy that all are equal by showing how poor low democracy's best are, and stooping to a level that aristocracy's servants would scorn...

Why do people get their sons letters published? Do the gentlefolk in England or France permit such a thing? You bet they don't. They value and treasure them and consider [them] secret if not sacred. The common people sometimes do but even they look down upon such things. One thing I will say. America's attitude has turned out a fine army of fighters. When they get into battle they fight to the finish because the people at home have shown them just how valuable life is.'[65]

Springs' nerves were clearly strained at this point as evidenced by his flight log entry of 23 September – '53 Fokkers. Plane all shot to hell,'[66] which no doubt affected his mood towards his parents, again chasing after an emotional component that he was never able to experience growing up; instead looking for it in the letters he received from Leroy and Lena:

'You and father seem to be so tickled about my being over here and yet you will not do but one thing for me. You send me money or its equivalent in small doses. But waste time or thought on me? Never. Cash in small amounts? Sure. Articles I write for. Yes possibly if it's not too much trouble. But sit down and think out something you can do for me, figure out something I would like to have, take time and write me decent letters regularly? Never.'[67]

Such was his frustration that Springs actually told his parents what he was looking for from their letters. He was not content with reality, he wanted a fictionalized, idealized version of his flesh and blood father and stepmother:

'Now sit down and write me that you are glad I'm at the front, glad I'm fighting and will continue fighting until they get me and when I am shot down you will rejoice with me that I have achieved a glorious end and regret only that I could not have postponed that end. And don't write me that you want my life spared at the expense of someone else's. If I do return let it be through my own skill.'[68]

AERO-NEUROSIS

The fighting continued at a fever pitch for Springs, each dogfight seemingly worse than the previous one:

> 'There are nineteen holes in my machine, two spars shot through, a bolt shot out of my propeller, and the machine generally scorched by inflammatory bullets. I didn't get hit myself but I could smell the phosphorous as the stuff went by...My machine is so badly shot up that I'm going to get a new one much as I hate to part with it...I've had to have seven new wings on it in the last three weeks.'[69]

Springs was taken off front line service; he was finished with flying in combat which gave rise to a whole host of new problems for him; the adrenaline-fuelled effect of combat flying was hard to relinquish, but he bore the scars. He never expected to survive the war, and now that he had, he had difficulty making the emotional adjustment.[70] He noted that while he was with the 148th he

> 'had a wheel shot off in the air. I shot my own prop off a dozen times, I had a little bomb stick to my undercarriage and I have been a nervous wreck ever since. I still wake up at night with the sound of screaming wires and the smell of brimstone. I have seen twenty pilots at dinner when the phone rang with orders for the dawn patrol. After they got the orders not a pilot could lift a glass to his mouth with one hand--ring a phone at dinner and they still can't.'[71]

Springs evidently suffered two relapses of some kind, the first, less debilitating, in Paris during the first half of October, during which he wrote the following letter to Leroy on 9 October in which he still suffered paradoxically from both nerves and his addiction to front line air fighting:

> 'I'm a complete and total nervous wreck though why I should be at this stage I can't figure. I'm a chattering idiot they tell me and I'm expecting my hair to turn gray daily. However, a little flying ought to soothe my nerves...I want a squadron, I want to be a major and I'm going to stay at the Front at all costs.'[72]

The second episode was much more serious and it occurred after the Armistice. From 13 November until 1 December, he had to go to the hospital, where he remained essentially immobilized for two weeks. One of the comments in his diary written on 15 November suggests that he was so distraught that he was considering suicide (by jumping out of a window). He wrote only one letter home during this period.[73]

Springs wrote the following epitaph to his wartime flying. It is tinged with bittersweet remorse over a never to be repeated chapter of his life, his 'crowded hour of glory' as Arthur Gould Lee described it. Springs noted that at the Front lay the 'biggest part of himself':

> 'There is no longer the "Front" there is no longer that place where every man is known by his merit, where a grim though sure justice prevails, and where there is always a haven of rest for those whom the world treats ill. Expiation is now withdrawn—everyone puts on their kid gloves. Pandora's box flies open again and Repentance and Remorse rush upon us.[74]
>
> 'No matter where I go or what I do, the best part of me will always remain between Zeebrugge and Armentieres, and in front of Cambrai. There I lived a life, a long lifetime, there lie my companions, and many adversaries and there also lies the biggest part of myself.
>
> 'I know every tree, every village, every road, every canal, every little wood, every little change of color between Nieuport and Roye for twenty miles on either rise of the lines...I've spent a couple of hundred hours up above it, look first down then up, searching below as well as above. I've flown between piles of ruins of Nieuport, Dixmunde, Ypres...and their memory will always be a sear.'[75]

After the war, Springs wrote his classic work *Warbirds – Diary of an Unknown Aviator*, which was an effort by him to memorialize his fallen friend John Grider; whose letters the book was ostensibly based upon, and to whom Springs attributed authorship. However, Grider's diary ended well before the story ended in *Warbirds* thus making Springs the true author of most of the book. Perhaps Springs wanted to create the ending for his wartime experiences that reality had deprived him; that Mac made it through that last summer of the war right alongside Callahan and himself, before finally being shot down. Just as he had told his father and stepmother how he wished they would behave towards him in reality, he was finally able, through the exacting process of writing, to portray the war and his comrades in a fashion he liked best. Undoubtedly, he felt cheated by the premature death of his friend. Moreover, by creating an expanded version of Mac's character in the book, he was able to share his feelings about the war without ascribing authorship of them to himself, which is both ingenious and must have been tremendously liberating. The true sentiments of Springs could now live as the words of Grider; thereby dodging the outright exploitation of his war letters (which he found so repugnant) and freeing him from the automatic and inescapable psychology of interacting with one's parents. Moreover, the composition of *Warbirds* could also have been conversations between the 'Three Musketeers' or other fliers in the squadron, forming a composite or synthetic story that resonated with all flyers of the Great War.

First Lieutenant John Grider and Springs were two of 210 cadets who joined the Aviation section of the US Army Signal Corps shortly after the US entered the First World War in 1917. The men from this group volunteered for service abroad and were sent to England to be trained. Grider, like Springs, was assigned to Squadron 85 under command of Billy Bishop in May 1918. When Grider was killed in action on 18 June. He had four victories to his credit. Grider wrote about his thoughts on his own mortality and atonement for 'wasted years' aboard the SS *Carmania*:

> 'I want to die well and not be killed in some accident or die of sickness – that would be terrible, a tragic anticlimax. I haven't lived very well but I am determined to die well…Thank God, I am going to have the opportunity to die as every brave man should wish to die – fighting – and fighting for my country as well. That would retrieve my wasted years and neglected opportunities.'[76]

This passage is very early in *Warbirds* and would appear different in tone from Spring's letters, including notions of atonement and the idea of a glorious death. However, the following passage in Springs' letter to his mother of 24 September 1918 echoes this sentiment: 'when I am shot down you will rejoice with me that I have achieved a glorious end and regret only that I could not have postponed that end'. The following passage adds an element of insecurity which could be attributed to Springs, Grider, or any number of aviators:

> 'When I think of all the good men that have been killed and then see all the bums that are still alive hanging around town, it makes me mad. Justice is blind, all right. And God is not fair

about it. Why should he take men like Fry and Stillman and Nathan and all the rest of the good ones and leave bums like me hanging around? It's not right. I feel sort of ashamed to be here still. I'll bet what the government owes me that I can name those that will be the survivors, if any, of our outfit.'[77]

The following passage is clever and rich in that it is Springs describing himself through Grider's eyes. He is clearly calling himself out regarding the acrimonious relationship with his father – the attribution has to be Elliott Springs as the villain in this passage is clearly Leroy – but in an act of contrition, the son shares some of the blame:

'Springs is all right until he gets mail from home, then he gets into a terrible rage and wants to fight the wide, wide world. He and his father seem to carry on a feud at long range. He's got so now he doesn't open any letters until after he's had a few drinks and some of them he doesn't open at all. His father writes him full details and instructions in triplicate about how to do everything and finds fault with everything he does. He showed me a couple of them and they certainly were nasty. Springs is no saint but he isn't nearly all that bad. I don't see why he cares what's going on at home. He worries about everything his father says and takes all his criticism to heart, tho why he should worry over it when he's three thousand miles away is beyond me. He's three thousand miles closer to hell. He must be awfully fond of his father to care what he thinks about things he doesn't know anything about. And the idea of losing sleep because someone three thousand miles away hasn't got sense enough to understand English when you write it to them, is absurd!'[78]

Springs continues the explanation of himself through Grider's eyes, crucifying his father for what he perceived as his father's chief motivation; being the father of a fallen war hero. The letters however, tell a different story. Leroy repeatedly cautions his son about being careful, a notion that originated in the Asheville school regarding sporting activities:

'We got to talking about home. He said that he had to get killed because he couldn't go home. He said if he got killed, his father would have a hero for a son and he could spend all his time and money building monuments to him and make himself very happy and proud. But if he lives through it and goes home, he says his father will fight with him for the rest of his life.'[79]

Springs' cynical description of how to make a movie to the filmmaker that visited his squadron may have been the inspiration for the following passage in *Warbirds*, although this is less subtle, more forthright. This is another fine example of how Springs was able to vent his true feelings through the persona of his fallen friend:

> 'What a nightmare this war is! I'm beginning to understand the term "Anti-Christ". Both the Allies and the Germans pray to the same God for strength in their slaughter! What a joke it must seem to Him to see us puny insignificant mortals proclaiming that we are fighting for Him and that He is helping us. Think of praying to the God of Peace for help in the War! The heavens must shake with divine mirth.'[80]

The following passage is from Springs' letter of 20 September to his stepmother:

> 'Of course, American people are proud that their men are fighting for what they think right (even though a lot had to be forced to) but at the same time they go about proclaiming it to the world, taking credit for it, boasting of it, advertising it, and endeavoring to transfer the pride in the soldier to the pride in one's self. Will American families wear the decorations, wound stripes, and service chevrons of their beloved also? Why not?'[81]

In contrast, the similar passage in *Warbirds* is a condensed, softened version of the same sentiment:

> 'An American Division was landing at Boulogne and these boys certainly have got funny ideas. They think they are crusaders and talk like headlines. They are full of catch-phrases and ideals. We talked to a bunch of them in the bar. They think they are on the way to a Sunday School picnic.'[82]

ELLIOTT WHITE SPRINGS – THE TRUE WAR BIRD

Springs' letters contain constant reference to his troubles with nerves; never does he attribute this to an excess of caffeine. Again, *Warbirds* offers a more accessible and palatable explanation for nerves:

> 'I got up this morning feeling like a week-end in the city though I had no reason to. I drank too much coffee before going up and I'm as nervous as a kitten now. Must be getting the Woofits.'[83]

The following passage is reminiscent of Mannock, as both complained about time on the ground as being worse than air fighting, the greatest fear lies in anticipation, so to speak. He does cleverly insert a passage from one of his letters into this passage:

> 'I have seen twenty pilots at dinner when the phone rang with orders for the dawn patrol. After they got the orders not a pilot could lift a glass to his mouth with one hand.'

The following is from Springs' letters of 24 August to his mother in which he states:

> 'And I'm getting so bored at being shot at that I don't bother to dodge anymore. I sat in the midst of Archie bursts yesterday for five minutes and yawned, refused to turn until they knocked me about thirty feet.'[84]

Now compare this to the passage in *Warbirds* ostensibly written by Grider:

> 'And I'm getting so bored at being shot at that I don't bother to dodge any more. I sat up in the middle of the Archie bursts yesterday for five minutes, yawned and refused to turn until they knocked me about a hundred feet. I used to be scared to death of Archie and gunfire from the ground. Now it almost fails to excite even my curiosity.'[85]

The text of *Warbirds* is littered with direct, indirect, and paraphrased passages from Springs' letters to his parents.

It is apparent that even during Springs' combat flying, he was thinking of writing what he considered a truthful accounting of air fighting during the

First World War. He does not refrain from showing his contempt for pulp or uninformed tracts on flying:

> 'We are going to form a new society – the Society for the Extermination of Amateur Aerial Authors – the purpose of which will be to protect the public from a flood of bunk.'[86]

Springs expanded his criticism to propaganda in the United States in general:

> 'It will never do to let the people at home find out the truth about this war. They've been fed on bunk until they'd never believe anything that didn't sound like a monk's story of the Crusades.'[87]

Interestingly, his inclusion of the Crusades reference which could be referencing Wilson, who was viewed as an idealistic crusader by many.

Springs also included some much-needed levity in *Warbirds*, even if it was the sort of black humour that many pilots such as Mannock practised:

> 'He [Springs] was not so good. He and Bim have had tombstones made for themselves. They are hollow and if they go down on the Hun side, they are to be filled with high explosive and dropped over, if they are killed on this side, they are to be filled with cognac so it will leak on them.'[88]

Springs' commentary on the desperate and murderous nature of combat by 1918 – gone forever were the traces of chivalry seen in the early years of the war:

> 'Hilary Rex has been killed. He was in a fight with a Fokker and his machine was disabled and he had to land. He landed all right and got out of his plane. The Hun dove on him and shot him as he was standing by his plane.'[89]

Both Mannock and Springs understood the corrosive nature of air combat all too well, that each man only had so much courage or emotional capital. It was a race against time to see if each man could make through the war honourably; some simply could not:

> 'One of our noblest he-men, a regular fire-eater to hear him tell it, has turned yellow at the front. He was quite an athlete

> and always admitted he was very hot stuff. He was ordered up on a bomb raid and refused to go. The British sent him back to American HQ with the recommendation that he be court-martialed for cowardice. He would have been too, if his brother hadn't been high up on the A.E.F. staff. He pulled some bluff about the machines being unsafe and they finally sent him home as an instructor and promoted him.'[90]

As with Lambert, Mannock, Springs, Udet, and countless other aviators, the addictive desire to continue fighting while paradoxically being neurasthenic was preponderant. Springs' insight into the nature and pathology of fear, was especially germane:

> 'But we've lost a lot of good men. It's only a question of time until we all get it. I'm all shot to pieces. I only hope I can stick it. I don't want to quit. My nerves are all gone and I can't stop. I've lived beyond my time already. It's not the fear of death that's done it. I'm still not afraid to die. It's this eternal flinching from it that's doing it and has made a coward out of me. Few men live to know what real fear is. It's something that grows on you, day by day, that eats into your constitution and undermines your sanity. I have never been serious about anything in my life and now I know that I'll never be otherwise again…Here I am, twenty-four years old, I look forty and feel ninety. I've lost all interest in life beyond the next patrol.'[91]

Springs' pessimism peaked at the close of the war. Giving his voice to an expanded version of Grider enabled him to express his innermost thoughts on the struggle in which he was engaged:

> 'The worst thing about this war is that it takes the best. If it lasts long enough the world will be populated by cowards and weaklings and their children. And the whole thing is so useless so unnecessary, so terrible! Even those that live through it will never be fit for anything else.'[92]

The last sentence is very reminiscent of Mannock, Udet, Remarque, and many others, the notion of irreversible transformation that occurred during the war experience. Springs thought he would eventually receive word that

AERO-NEUROSIS

Grider was safe, either in a hospital or in a German prison camp and he stubbornly clung to hope. Alternatively, it was a coping mechanism that enabled him to carry on:

> 'But when you lunch with a man, talk to him, see him go out and get in his plane in the prime of his youth and the next day someone tells you that he is dead – it just doesn't sink in and you can't believe it. And the oftener it happens the harder it is to believe. I've lost over a hundred friends, so they tell me – I've seen only seven or eight killed – but to me they aren't dead yet. They are just around the corner, I think, and I'm still expecting to run into them any time.'[93]

With death all around him, and his own death squarely on his mind, like so many others, Springs had to believe that 'Surely the human life is not a candle to be snuffed out'.[94] He also made the observation that 'The English have all turned spiritualistic since the war'. Belief in some sort of afterlife or larger existential framework had become a necessary coping mechanism as so many men had died such horrible deaths, those that were still living tried to find something hopeful to cling to.

Springs ended *Warbirds* at this point noting that it was due to the death of its author John Grider, in aerial combat, but in reality, he was shot down in June 1918. *Warbirds* claimed he was shot down by a German plane twenty miles behind the German lines but in reality how he died is unclear. He was given a decent burial by the Germans and his grave was later found by the Red Cross. Springs undoubtedly carried his memory with him for the rest of his days.

After the war, Springs begrudgingly cast himself in the role his father wanted most; to take over the family business, The Springs' textile mills in Lancaster, South Carolina. He was a successful businessman but continued to suffer from his relationship with Leroy and the war. In a letter to his wife, Frances, he wrote that according to one psychiatrist:

> 'The doctor says I have been behind the eight ball all my life and this is the first chance I've had to shake off my nervousness...[He] predicts great things when I absorb his teachings in mental hygiene...he told me that it was time I quit trying to cure myself and let him cure me. He says I had a genuine war neurosis after 1918 and that I apparently cured

ELLIOTT WHITE SPRINGS – THE TRUE WAR BIRD

myself by writing it out, but that I didn't have the concrete foundation under me to prevent its return…my troubles are rooted in 1918 and in Father.'[95]

Springs obviously had an active imagination which, as Anderson noted, was responsible for great suffering during aerial combat; however, that same imagination helped him recover from his trauma.

Chapter 8

The Slow Fuse – William Lambert

William Lambert was born in Ohio in 1894. He became a chemist at a steel works, and, eager to take part in the First World War, in 1915 he travelled to Canada to work in a munitions factory. In late 1916 he decided to take a more active part in the war and volunteered for the Royal Flying Corps, pursuing a love of flying that he had held since his first flight in 1910.

After training in Toronto, Lambert was sent to Europe and in March 1918, he joined No.24 Squadron, flying S.E 5a fighters in France, just in time for Operation Michael, the German Spring Offensive in late March. It was a hectic period as the Germans were breaking through the Western Front and, like Springs, Lambert was involved in strafing and bombing as well as reconnaissance and dogfighting in an effort to stem the German advance. On 7 April, Lambert got his first victory, an Albatros DV. Over the coming months, he would claim at least another 17 victories, receiving a Distinguished Flying Cross after his tenth.

The following seems to have been the norm in many British squadrons; it was considered in bad taste outwardly to express fear or seem to be sulking. The fatalism that was prevalent is also described:

> 'At lunch...a lot of kidding and boisterous horseplay took place. Good humor prevailed. Life was good but would we all be around those tables at supper time? There was always an element of fear deep in every man there but very few allowed this to come to the surface. Most of us face the fact that: what is to be, will be.'[1]

In Henry Armstrong's book *Aviation Medicine,*[2] he wrote that inspiration for flying stemmed from religion, an obvious reflection of his own norms.

THE SLOW FUSE – WILLIAM LAMBERT

A more common and believable explanation is described by Lambert; birds – not chickadees or finches; but raptors:

> 'I always watched those birds with wide-spread wings coming through the air as easily as I could walk on the ground. How I wished I could do that. Little did I then know that within a few years, I would achieve this aim. But my mission would not be for food. No! I should be gliding down to kill my fellow man.'[3]

Lambert provides us with a unique anthropomorphic description of the bond formed by the one thing that could insure his survival in combat; his plane. He describes the marriage between pilot and machine that resulted in an effective fighting unit:

> '1084 [his S.E.5a] was also ready and going well. If an aeroplane did not respond instantly and transmit its every vibration to me we never became a successful flying unit. I felt that I should know and feel every whim, mood and temperament of a plane. Without that, you were nothing and neither would survive long. I worked constantly with 1084; adjusted this, readjusted that, checked carburetors and magnetos, lengthened this wire, shortened that. I pulled the Vickers apart, went over every part and oiled and reassembled it. The same with the Lewis. I guess I drove my A.M.s crazy. But 1084 was as near perfect as we could make her. This may sound crazy but it was the way I felt.'[4]

With so little within the realm of individual control in combat, fine tuning one's plane was a way a pilot could do something tangible to improve his odds and the notion of the plane being a living, breathing thing that needed attention is also compelling and understandable. The same affection sailors had for their vessels, pilots had for their 'ships' as well, especially during this period when planes, like sailing ships, were made from canvas and wood. A sage mariner once noted that something went out of the navy when it changed from sail to steam; the same could be said about aircraft of this period relative to subsequent all-metal aircraft. They were challenging to fly, and mastering that challenge gave the aviator tremendous satisfaction and pride.

AERO-NEUROSIS

Lambert noted that good cheer, boisterousness, and other antics helped keep pilots from focusing on the reality of their situation. He was thankful for his youth:

> 'When one is so pliable that a pleasant and sometimes a trifling event completely removes all morose thoughts. In war flying, brooding did no one any good. Too many good pilots were lost due to this.'[5]

The fact that he was cognizant of this phenomenon leads one to believe that he brooded about it occasionally.

Like Springs, Lambert hated strafing. It must be understood that this was a completely new tactic in an already new context; dogfighting was only a few years old and that was stressful enough. Now, during the mobile phase of the war, the air forces had become an extension of the army, whereas before they had been an extension of artillery observation:

> 'At 600 feet he levelled off and headed for a small wooded area...now I saw Daley's target. In a battered trench about half a mile long, 300 to 400 Germans were sheltering. I saw helmets and backs as they crouched there with rifles in hands. Those poor devils were helpless. What a slaughter it would be. They were human beings and I wondered could I do it? ... I went in firing both guns...one poor devil tried to pull a piece of sheet metal over his body; some lay flat; some crouched with faces looking up at me; one big fellow defiantly stood up straight with a rifle to a shoulder...incidents like this sometimes made me want to quit. How I hated this aspect of our work. Guess I was just not made for it.'[6]

Seemingly, Lambert was in need of a rest, now a familiar tactic in the RFC for preventing a pilot from cracking up when becoming even slightly symptomatic. Again, the bond with 1084 is obvious. He checks on his mount in a similar way a cavalryman might look after his horse:

> 'A beautiful morning. Bright sun and not a cloud in the sky. What a day for flying. Probably plenty of E.A. to be found this morning. What the hell is wrong with me? I am not flying today. I am on my way to London. No more flying for at least

two weeks. Off to the hangar to take a look at 1084. There she sits, well back in a corner of the hangar. Let's hope she stays there for my period of leave. A short hop around the field right now would be nice. I am sure going to miss this.'[7]

After Lambert returned to Conteville from leave, he discovered that his good friend Daley was dead. This was the final shock that lit the fuse to his eventual breakdown:

'Daley was gone forever. What happened? I asked him. He had a bad accidental crash on July 7 and died in the hospital the next day. That hit me hard. Other pilots had been killed during my time but none of them had been close to me so I never gave their deaths much thought. But Daley was different. We thought alike. We had been almost like brothers for three months and had worked together as a team of two. He had driven the enemy off my tail many times and I had done the same for him. I can see him even now, on patrol, after doing something that pleased him. He would move in close to me, wingtip to wingtip, look over and wave to me with a wide grin covering his face. During the time we were together I never knew him take a negative outlook on life. Yes, I would certainly miss Daley. The sad news just about "knocked me for a loop"....I could not get Daley off my mind.'[8]

Lambert went through the motions of being back at his squadron, though he continued to grieve over the loss of his friend. After dinner he played a game with his friend Palmer; but his mind was not on the game; he could not help how he felt:

'With darkness we could see the flashes on the skyline like summer lightening. Palmer beat me as I could not keep my mind on the game for thinking of Daley. That was something that I had to stop. I took a chair next to Selwyn who told me to take the next day off to rest up from my leave.'[9]

Armstrong wrote that 'the longer a man is away from his unit the more difficult it is for him to successfully return to combat.'[10] This notion is very evident in the following passage from Lambert shortly after he returned to 24 Squadron from leave:

> 'I eased the throttle forward and 1084 started to roll; full throttle now, a few bumps and we were in the air. How could my sixteen days of absence have made things seem so unusual? Back on the throttle and a climb to about 1500 feet. That's better; my confidence is returning...'[11]

On the morning of 8 August, the date of the big combined allied offensive, Lambert went on a strafing patrol with Selywn and Harries, Hellett, Wren, and Bair. Their objective was the area around Rosieres.[12] During this flight, Lambert's fuel tank was punctured due to groundfire forcing him to land – twice. Finally, he had to abandon his beloved 1084:

> 'I jump out and run towards them (allied cavalry) as the Germans start to shell 1084. I run back to her, reach into the cockpit and by some super-human effort manage to get the watch from her dashboard. (that watch now occupies an honoured spot on the wall of my bedroom with other trophies). I stand beside her briefly, just thinking. Farewell 1084. You have pulled me out of many a tight spot and have never let me down. Now we must part.'[13]

As with Springs, this offensive was a busy and arduous time for the RAF as they were charged with close ground support of the advance. As noted with Springs, the frequency and danger of these missions took their toll:

> 'After yesterday the nerves of almost every pilot in the squadron were about shot. Most had been doing this work for three weeks. No one complained but one had only to look into the face of a pilot and watch his actions. The story was there. During the fighting of the previous day I had no time to think about it but 24 hours later it was a different story.'[14]

Lambert commented that for the past month (most of July) his flight had done all of their many missions with only six pilots: Selywn, Bair, Hellett, Harries, Wren and himself that none of them had any rest, and that they flew all patrols.[15] On an afternoon patrol they encounter several flights of Germans; Albatrosses, Fokker D. VIIs, one Pfalz D.III, two Hannoveraners and one Halberstadt (two seater):

> 'Soon the sky's whole arc is one mass of flying machines. Twelve S.E.5s and eighteen Germans. Oh! If I only had 1084 with me. I am not sure of this new plane.'[16]

At this point in Lambert's narrative combat fatigue has set in, only he did not really know it yet: 'C flight had no spare aeroplanes, so I could not rejoin the patrol and, frankly, I did not regret this too much and was well satisfied to stay on the ground.'[17] This was seemingly the first evidence that Lambert was suffering consciously. His subconscious was on a fast track that finally caused a massive breakdown, like a switch turning off:

> 'Almost everything from that day until about October 1, 1918 is a blank. I do not know what happened to me, only that I was suffering from trouble with my ears and, possibly, the effects of combat fatigue. However, certain incidents are remembered dimly...I vaguely remember the raid and seeing the fires. And I know Alex Mathews was killed at the time. My recollection is of watching someone loading my gear into a tender. Later, I was swimming with another pilot on a long white, sandy beach. Before going into the water I folded my large bath towel in a neat bundle. A very small French bulldog was playing on the beach and when I returned I found that the dog had left his calling card right in the center of my towel.'[18]
>
> 'A woman in nurse's uniform, strolling along the beach, joined us and asked if we would like to go up to a large building on the cliff top. She told us that it was a resort hotel – at Wimereux – and had been converted into a hospital. We were patients there. This puzzled us. What were we doing there? Later I was in a London hospital, evidently for the whole of September. Two things stand out in my mind of the stay there. First of being attended by two doctors. One had a slender, flexible wire contraption about twelve inches long and to which was attached an electric cord. This wire was inserted into, and pushed half way up, one of my nostrils and it was explained as part of the treatment to the ruptured ear drums I had apparently contracted... I seem to recall enduring this

most painful and extremely unpleasant torture about every second or third day for period of several weeks…About the last week of September I was told that if I wished I could go home at my own expense for three months leave. You can bet that "I wished".'[19]

William Lambert was admitted to the Queen Alexandra's Hospital in Millbank, London on 27 August 1918.[20] During the war, it had become a general hospital for the army and was next to the Tate Gallery. Apart from the casualties caused by ordnance, cases of trench fever, frostbite, shell-shock, and gas gangrene were treated here. Tens of thousands of wounded passed through QAH, the lights in the operating theatres never went out as doctors and nurses worked tirelessly to save as many as they could. Many expected there to be strict military discipline in this hospital; instead, they found 'only devotion, unremitting care and kindness'. After the war, many wrote letters thanking the medical staff for the care they received.

For Lambert, the war ended before he recovered fully, bringing his trauma to a close. Lambert emerged from the war with quite a souvenir; a piece of red linen from von Richthofen's Fokker Dr. 1 triplane. He was given leave to Canada on 30 August for three months and was demobilized on 30 September 1919.

Lambert's post-war life comprised a little barnstorming and working as an engineer in and around his hometown of Ironton, Ohio. He served with the Army Air Forces in the Second World War, retiring in 1954 as a lieutenant colonel in the U.S. Air Force. He died in 1982 aged 87.

Chapter 9

Besting the Baron – Roy Brown

Roy Brown grew up in the small town of Carlton Place, Ontario, Canada. His parents, Morton and Mary, provided a stable family environment due to Morton being a prosperous business man in their town. Roy loved sports – hockey and baseball – and would duck out of school to take swims with his friends in the river that ran past the school.[1] In 1911, the aviation bug was planted in Roy's mind when his uncle Clarence told him stories of daredevil feats and crashes of the Chicago Air Meet; Roy was fascinated.

He wrote a letter to his father on 11 April 1915 explaining his decision to go to war:

> '...I have never said so before but my reason for wanting military training was to go to the war. I have thought it over a long time and have come to the conclusion that it is my duty to go. This is no sudden burst of patriotism or a thirst for adventure or as you used to say, "fightin' and killin' and things". This war is a terribly serious thing and if we are to win we have to get large numbers of men to enlist...voluntarily...I have considered what it will mean to you at home and to myself. But where things like this are concerned, self has to be put aside and we need to look a little wider and broader...'[2]

As with any parents contemplating the untimely death of their son, they were not pleased with Roy's decision. However, recognizing his son's resolve found a niche he hoped his son would take with the Royal Naval Air Service (RNAS) which flew patrols against German Zeppelins and aircraft attacking Britain; it appeared far safer than the slaughter of the Western Front.

After graduating from Victoria High School, Roy, along with several others, was interviewed by Admiral Kingsmill at Naval Service HQ in Ottawa. Kingsmill was satisfied with the educational requirements and promised if they showed an aptitude for flying, they were eligible for further training in England, resulting eventually in commissions as probationary flight sub-lieutenants.[3]

Roy received his flight training from the Wright School of Aviation in Dayton, Ohio in 1915. Despite the impressive title, the school was not among the best in the world any more due to Orville's apathy over the school and his efforts to sell the entire company.[4] The school still used the basic Wright *Flyer* (Wright model B), a design that was by this time obsolete, when compared with other aircraft like the Bleriot IX, Deperdussin monoplane, and the Curtiss JN series of tractor biplanes.

Brown wrote to his mother in mid-September about life at Huffman Prairie:

> 'Time surely does fly here. Several of the fellows have bad colds. Stearne has had one ever since the first night we slept in the hangar. I think they are caused by our being in damp shoes all day caused by walking through the wet grass, and our bed clothes seem to be damp the majority of the time. The roof leaks pretty badly but my bed is in a dry place…I am going to…have a good Christian bath at the YMCA. I have not had one since the day we arrived and as the hangar is dirty and the work is dirty, you can imagine what we feel like…I like flying very much…'[5]

The class size began to gradually increased and the weather turned colder in October making camp life in the hangars miserable. The course dragged on due to a now large class size, only two aircraft, and inability to fly the Wright B's in anything other than perfectly calm conditions. Roy completed his course and waited to take his test to receive his Aero club certificate. On attempting this, he crashed the *Flyer* on 18 October due to a problem with the throttle mechanism.[6] Orville then demanded a $500 bond before Brown took his next certification flight, dragging the process out even further. He finally passed his test on 13 November 1915.

Probationary Sub-lieutenant Brown RNAS sailed for Britain aboard the SS *Finland* on 2 December 1915. He arrived at Chingford aerodrome,12 miles north of London, for training just before Christmas. He trained on Maurice Farman S7 Longhorns. On 12 February, Brown was promoted to advanced training stage, flying Avro 500, 540B, and 540C two-seaters.[7] On 17 February 1916 Brown wrote to his family back home:

> 'We are busier than ever though as they are making us pass exams in engines, Morse code, semaphore signaling, navigation, armament – which is a big subject, aeroplane construction and I don't know what else. All are pretty stiff examinations so you can see what we are up against…there is a rumour…that all the officers in this service who do not go onto seaplanes will be transferred to the Royal Flying Corps…I am not keen about seaplanes…I would much sooner go to France…although that is much more dangerous, I would prefer it. I guess it will be rather a nervous job with 8 inch…shells breaking under you…'[8]

Brown could not know how prophetic his comment about nerves would be. On 2 April, he began training in a BE2C. Nicknamed 'The Quirk',[9] Brown was hospitalized for a slight back injury for May and June and left on 11 July for a month's leave. In early August, he was back at Chingford to complete his training. After 39 hours and 46 minutes of flying time he was awarded his RNAS pilot's certificate no. 163 on 6 September. Three weeks of gunnery school at Eastchurch was next.[10] He was posted to RNAS Dover on 29 September, but his back injury returned and he was sent to Sheerness sick quarters, thus cancelling his posting. He returned to Eastchurch then back in Royal Naval hospital at Chatham by Christmas with tonsillitis. It would seem that Brown was prone to ailments. On 13 February 1917, Brown began training on Nieuports 10s and 12s at Dover.[11] On 9 March, he was released for transfer to an active squadron. The notes on his release were: 'Total time in air 45 hrs. Fairly ready for active service. More practice required.'[12] He was posted to Naval 9 squadron at Saint Pol aerodrome flying Sopwith Pups and Nieuport 11's. The job of the 9th was to protect Dunkirk harbours from enemy aircraft attacks, as well as defending Britain against marauding German bombers or zeppelins. Roy overturned a Pup on landing, which left him hospitalized for all of 'Bloody April' – luckily for him – as the RFC and RNAS lost about a third of their combined strength during this month alone.[13] His injury from the Pup accident exacerbated an old knee injury which meant returning to England for treatment. He was discharged in late April and posted to Walmer (between Dover and Deal on the South coast of England). He liked it here very much although noted:

> 'That is the big advantage of the air service. Your work is more a nervous strain than anything else and while it is on there is plenty of it but it does not last long and the rest of the time you have more or less to yourself…'[14]

AERO-NEUROSIS

On 10 May 1917, Brown was back at Saint Pol flying Pups on escort patrols (DH4s). Above 15,000 feet the Pups could outfly (due to light wing loading) the Albatros D. III which was the new German front line fighter. On 3 June, he was posted to Naval 11 at Hondeshoote Aerodrome, where due to the losses of Bloody April, he was placed in charge of a flight.[15] He also began flying Sopwith triplanes at this time, which by all accounts was a delightful aircraft. On 13 June, Brown was sent to Naval 4 squadron at Bray Dunes. He wrote to his mother on 29 June and according to Alan Bennett, author of *Roy Brown*, was at this time under strain due to the amount of trivia in his letter.[16] In a letter of 2 July, Brown confides that:

> 'Our work over here is very interesting and also exciting but it is rather risky at times. When you think about it afterwards you get afraid but at the time you are too busy to be afraid or anything else but concentrate on the work at hand.'[17]

This sentiment is consistent with other pilot reports such as Mannock about idle time. It is also evident that Brown was prone to contemplation and introspection. The waiting between actions provided time for self-evaluation and apprehension, both of which could erode the confidence so crucial to air fighting. On 4 July, Brown was transferred back to 11 squadron. On the 15th, he wrote to his father regarding his duties as flight commander 'You are in trouble about things the whole time but it's all in a day's work'.[18] On 17 July, south-east of Nieuport, Brown got his first victory; an Albatros D. III.[19] By this time, he was competent at his craft. The following is an account of a dogfight:

> '...we ran right into about eight of their scouts. I was right in the middle of them before I knew it. I opened fire on one and just got a few rounds off when he went down in a spin and my gun jambed [sic]. I cleared my jamb and opened fire on another one. I got a lot of lead into him and he went out of control immediately. He went down side-slipping every way but the right way. Then my gun jambed [sic] again and a Hun got under my tail, i.e. the back of my machine, and opened fire on me. I side-looped immediately and came out of the loop right on his tail and got about 25 rounds into him when he went down in a spin also. My gun jambed [sic] again, which I cleared, but there were no Huns left to fight with...came back

across the line dodging their anti-aircraft fire…they must have fired 75 shells at me but I stunted all around and got away alright…It surely is exciting while it lasts but I was scared stiff coming back through their Archie. It was much too close for comfort I can tell you.'[20]

The intensity of the patrols during June and July, which included many high altitude flights, as this gave the Pups tactical advantage, caused Brown to report sick by around 29 July when he wrote to his father:

'I have been on the sick list for a couple of days with my stomach. I feel O.K. again today though. My C.O. is as nice to me as he could be. Comes in and talks to me as if I were his own son…This is a rather unhealthy service to be in here at present but I am as careful as I can be. The trouble is when you are on the ground you make all kinds of good resolutions about how careful you will be but when you get in the air you feel altogether different and forget about them.'[21]

On 11 August, Brown wrote to his mother:

'I nearly crashed on landing as…I could not get it [engine] to start again. I was all in when I got down again as I was so scared. It's no fun, I can tell you. That is why I do not like writing about what we do as it is all done with too narrow a margin.'[22]

Brown was hospitalized briefly due to a re-emergence of his tonsillitis, but upon being discharged, found he was posted to Naval squadron 9 at Leffrinchouchke, which was fortuitous as his friend Stearne Edwards was there and he would be flying Sopwith Camels. Cole Palin wrote that 'Sopwith Camels were not difficult to fly, just different. The trick was to learn how to handle the differences before one of them killed you.'[23] The following is a somewhat humorous first verse and chorus of the 1917 Camel pilot's song:

The Camel is a noble bird,
Complete with wings and a hump
It flies about like any scout
And then it comes down with a bump.

AERO-NEUROSIS

Oh where, oh where have my two wheels gone?
Oh where, oh where can they be?
They're not around upon the ground,
They're up in the air, don't you see?[24]

The following log entry by Brown on 3 September simply stated 'First flip on a Clerget Camel. Do not like them.'[25] Brown eventually survived the training period in the Camel, unlike so many others, and began to see its strengths, one of which was its ability to spin readily to shake an enemy pursuer from one's tail: 'Hun dove on my tail and opened fire. I spun away. One hit in centre of right wing.'[26] By 9 September, Brown had his fifth victory; a two-seater. However, the British did not celebrate aces in the way other countries did so the event occurred with little ceremony or notice. Brown's father sent him a newspaper clipping of another flyer's exploits in the RFC; which like Springs, Roy did not like:

> '...you said something about wanting to publish some of my letters. I wrote once about that kind of thing when there was something in the *Citizen* and I feel more strongly against it now than I ever did. If you have noticed, it is the chaps who do nothing that put those in. They are all talk...when I write letters home they are for the family only. I do not care a rap whether people think I am doing anything or not. I am doing my best and can do no more.'[27]

Roy was a little outspoken on RNAS matters in several letters and sometimes by-passed the censor by posting letters in England. If even a hint of this reached the RNAS office in Ottawa, it would probably be reported to London, and that would spell trouble for him.[28] By mid-September, Brown wrote that 'everyone is feeling tired out and I hope we are able to carry on.' Later in the same letter he stated that he wished he could tell all that happens at the Front; obviously there was a lot more that was left unsaid than explicitly stated, be they for reasons of censorship or an impossibility for those at home to understand what these pilots were experiencing. By early October Roy admits to the intensity of what he has been going through:

> 'This is a day off for me, in fact for everyone, as it is raining and low clouds. I hope it keeps up for a week. This is the kind

BESTING THE BARON – ROY BROWN

of weather everyone likes to see. There has not been very much excitement the last few days but I have already had enough to last me the rest of my life...'[29]

Brown went on home leave from 11 November 1917 to mid-January 1918, arriving at Carlton Place around the end of November.[30] He and Stearnes left for Washington DC on 17 December to provide expert input to the US Navy regarding the protection of ships by aircraft, as well as providing input on the nature of the Belgian coastline. The US Navy was preparing plans to blockade the coast of Belgium and Germany but needed information about how best to protect ships as well as airfields (Ostend and Zeebrugge) with aircraft, something Brown and Stearnes and the RNAS squadron 4 knew something about.[31] When Brown and Stearnes returned, they found Naval 9 equipped with the latest Camels which featured the 150 hp Bentley, and hydraulic actuating gear for the twin Vickers machine guns, thus increasing rate of climb and reducing overheating and reducing the frequency of gun jams. The timing was perfect as soon the (improved) Fokker Dr. 1s would begin appearing in strength at the Front.[32]

Brown went on leave again shortly after his return from home leave. This was standard operating procedure for pilots exhibiting symptoms of combat fatigue. On 1 April, the RFC and the RNAS were combined to form the RAF. Apparently, this caused some acrimony as top leadership positions were to go to RFC men, subordinating those in the RNAS.[33] By this time, Russia had dropped out of the war, and Germany was planning a big offensive – 'Operation Michael' – at dawn on 21 March 1918. Forty German divisions began an advance across the plains near Saint Quentin towards Sir Hubert Gough's Fifth Army; it was a fateful move. The offensive was intended to move northwest and seize the channel ports which supplied the allied forces. Hindenburg changed his mind and had his forces attack the whole British line north of the Somme, trying to push them into the sea. The Germans were under the impression that Allied forces were just as hungry as they were; during their advance they were shocked to find cellars full of wine, and much more food than they had imagined; this slowed the advance markedly! It also bought the Allies the time they needed to reinforce.

The offensive was stopped at Villers-Bretonneaux, to the east of Amiens. German airfields could not provide adequate air support for the advance as their bases grew further and further from the advancing vanguard. Brown

AERO-NEUROSIS

and his squadron were charged with ground strafing which, like Springs and Lambert he found repugnant. Roy wrote that after 1 April, his new RAF squadron would be 209 stationed at Clairmarais Nord, belonging to RAF 11 Wing, and he noted that he would be a Captain in the RAF as well.[34]

In early April, 209 squadron was moved to Bertangles aerodrome which was just north of Amiens and attached to 22 wing. Bertangles was also home to RAF 65,84,23 and 48 squadrons, as well as Australian Flying Corps 3 squadron. In mid-April von Richthofen's flying circus was moved to Cappy aerodrome, which was captured after the Allies retreated. The purpose of this move was to establish air superiority in the Hamel-Corbie-Amiens region. Brown's flight log records one of his first scraps with a Dr 1:

> 'Dived on 2 Fokker Triplanes. One did an Immelmann turn in front of me and I got in a good burst. He went down vertical and me after him. Burst in flame. Carried on vertical then pulled out and I left him at 500' gliding as if pilot was dead and machine naturally stable. Went down near Warfusse-Abancourt.'[35]

That night Bertangles and Poulanville aerodromes were bombed, depriving the pilots of any sleep. Food was short, due to the supply route being shelled by German artillery. Brown ate (rancid) rabbit for his noon meal and came down with food poisoning; he was sent to 41 Stationary Hospital in the village of Bertangles.[36] He returned to the aerodrome on the 15th, although still unwell. Their aerodrome was now being shelled and bombed, the lack of sleep from which exacerbated Brown's condition. He was now living on milk and brandy. On 20 April, Raymond Collishaw visited his friend Brown – both were former RNAS pilots. Brown's and Collishaw's Squadrons were stationed close to one another so Collishaw paid him a visit. The following is Collishaw's description of Brown who:

> 'Remembered a handsome, black-haired, square-jawed pilot full of joy for flying. The man he found that afternoon was utterly different. There were gray hairs in his head, he lost 25 pounds and his once sparkling eyes were now bloodshot and sunken in his face. Brown admitted he been living for more than a month on a diet of milk and Brandy. He said he had already had a nervous breakdown and that he was suffering from a severe ulcer. Collishaw was shocked and

BESTING THE BARON – ROY BROWN

begged his friend not to fly any further missions. Both men knew this was impossible.'[37]

The next day dawned just like any other; it would become Roy's claim to fame; his encounter with Baron Manfred von Richthofen. His log from April 21, 1918 reads:

> '21.4.18-9:30 am – Camel B7270 – 90 mins. – H.O.P. –
> (1) Observed 2 seater Albatross shot down in flames by Lieut. Taylor.
> (2) Dived on large formation of triplanes and Albatros single-seaters. Two triplanes got on my tail so I cleared off. Climbed up and got back to scrap. Dived on pure red triplane which was on Lieut. May's tail. Got in good burst when he went down. Observed to crash by Lieut. Mellersh and Lieut. May. Dived on two more triplanes which were chasing Lieut. Mellersh. Did to them. Red triplane was Baron von Richthofen, confirmed by medical examination after being claimed by Australian RE8 squadron and 11th Australian Brigade.'[38]

Seemingly there was some doubt in Roy's mind as to who actually shot Richthofen down as evidenced by his wording of 'when he went down', meaning that he added a burst to perhaps others who fired the fatal shot. Bennett argues that he used the word 'when' instead of 'whereupon' in a log entry on 22 March; however, this is highly speculative.[39] The 11th Australian Infantry Brigade, and the 14th Australian Field Artillery Brigade also claimed credit for the Baron's death. The rumour was at the time that Sgt Cedric B. Popkin of the 11th Brigade had fired on the Red Baron; by nightfall the 14th brigade was claiming credit made by gunners Buie and Evans.[40]

Lieutenant May's logbook contains the following entry describing the famous encounter:

> '21.4.18 – Camel D3326 – 90 mins – Engaged 15 to 20 triplanes. Claimed one blue one. Several on my tail. Came out with red triplane on my tail which followed me down to the ground and over the lines on my tail all the time. Got several bursts into me but didn't hit me. When we got across the lines he was shot down by Captain Brown. I saw him crash into side of hill. Came back

AERO-NEUROSIS

with Capt. We afterwards found out that the triplane (red) was the famous German airman Baron Richtofen. He was killed.'[41]

In spite of the ground fire claims, the RAF gave Roy official credit for a Fokker Dr. 1 near Vaux-sur-Somme. May would later confess that he did not actually see Brown attack the Baron's triplane. Moreover, a corporal gunner on an R.E.8 of AFC 3 squadron also claimed credit for the red triplane. The responsibility for salvaging wrecked aircraft in the area covered by 22 Wing – Allied or German – fell to AFC 3. The duty of collecting the wreckage of von Richthofen's triplane fell to Walter Warneford:

'Von Richtofen down at sheet 62D J 19b 4.4 Salved[salvaged] the a/c and von Richtofen's body under their fire. Arived back with body at 7:10 hrs. and returned. Brought in the a/c getting back at 12:30 midnight. Later it was found that Gunner Buer [Buie] of the Australian Artillery had shot him from the ground.'[42]

After his morning patrol on 22 April, Brown visited the tent in which the body of the fallen Baron was resting. This excerpt is from a letter to his mother:

'... the sight of Richthofen as I walked closer gave me a start. He appeared so small to me, so delicate. He looked so friendly. Blond, silk-soft hair, like that of a child, fell from the broad, high forehead. His face, particularly peaceful, had an expression of gentleness and goodness, of refinement. Suddenly I felt miserable, desperately unhappy, as if I had committed an injustice. With a feeling of shame, a kind of anger against myself moved in my thoughts, that I had forced him to lay there. And in my heart I cursed the force that is devoted to death. I gnashed my teeth, I cursed the war. If I could I would gladly have brought him back to life, but that is somewhat different than shooting a gun. I could no longer look him in the face. I went away. I did not feel like a victor. There was a lump in my throat. If he had been my dearest friend, I could not have felt greater sorrow.'[43]

Roy Brown was a decent man who could not keep his humanity at bay any longer. After seeing the dead Baron he felt ashamed; hiding behind pro-war rhetoric would not cut it for him any longer. He saw von Richthofen as simply a man, no more no less, that he had killed.

In the morning of 22 April, Colonels Sinclair and Nixon examined the Baron's body which was inconclusive. The bullet had entered from the side which basically meant that the fatal slug could not have been fired by Buie, Evans, or Brown.[44] Another medical examination was conducted by Colonel Barber of the Australian Corps, and his aide Major Chapman. They agreed with the entry and exit points ascribed by Sinclair and Nixon but went on to say that the shot could have been fired from the ground at a banking aircraft.[45] Sgt Popkin of 24 Machine Gun company filed a claim on 21 April but was set aside due to pressing tactical military concerns.

The bombing and shelling of Bertangles aerodrome continued, and Roy did not fly on the 23rd due to 'stomach trouble'. On 27 April, he wrote to his father about his condition:

> '...I feel just about all in today the way things have gone. My stomach has been very bad recently and the doctor says if I keep on I shall have a nervous break-down and has ordered me to stop active service flying. I am to have two weeks leave and then go up for a medical examination again. I have done everything in my power to come back to France after that but it does not look very hopeful.'[46]

He continues in his letter about his encounter with von Richthofen:

> '...It was the most terrible fight I have ever seen in the air. I doubt whether there has been one like it before. We shot down three of their triplanes, which were seen to crash and one that has not been confirmed as yet. Among these was the Baron whom I shot down on our side of the lines.'[47]

Brown finished his letter by commenting on the debate surrounding who actually shot the Baron down. His letter to his father is less explicit than the one to his mother yet the profound effect this event had on Brown is evident:

> 'It was rather funny about Richthofen being shot down... all reports differed. They had a medical examination on the body and it was found that they were all wrong without the

slightest doubt. It is terrible when you think of it that they should examine a body to see who should have the credit of killing him. What I saw that day shook me up quite a lot as it was the first time I have ever seen a man whom I knew I had killed. If you don't shoot them they will shoot you so it has to be done.'[48]

These last two sentences are in microcosm the essence of much of the trauma experienced by First World War flyers: when they confronted their victims in this previously 'faceless war' they were deeply moved; yet, they continued to parrot back their training regarding the ethos of 'kill or be killed'. It is obvious that the dissonance created by these two sentiments would ultimately yield trauma. Moreover, Brown did not seem to take any pleasure in shooting down the Baron. John T. McCurdy stressed the importance of sublimation in enabling men to kill without qualms:

'The sensitive individual who cannot develop a pleasure in killing – to put the matter brutally – is bound to be a victim of double strain, and quickly develops an unconquerable hatred of the task that will soon lead to fear. Once fear appears, surrender or illness is the only escape.'[49]

On 30 April, Brown was sent to 24 General Hospital, Etaples for treatment and rest. The encounter with the Red Baron was the final straw, as he was perennially sick, tired, and suffering from nervous exhaustion. On 1 May, he was recommended for the DSO for 'conspicuous gallantry and devotion to duty'.

Brown was discharged from 24 General Hospital on 16 May. The leadership decided it was high time he received a long rest, so he was sent to England for a fortnight. The medical reasons given for this decision revolve around physiological factors such as hypoxia and cold but make no mention of his psychological state. For the next few months he would serve as an instructor at an advanced school for fighter pilots at the Home Establishment (H.E.). No. 2 School of Aerial Fighting at Marske-by-the-Sea, Yorkshire.[50] Perhaps of equal importance, Brown was now a national treasure; the RAF pilot who had shot down the Red Baron. It simply would not do to have him exposed to combat any more where he could in turn be bested by another (potentially lesser) German pilot.

BESTING THE BARON – ROY BROWN

After a brief taste of freedom in London, Roy ended up in RAF General Hospital (Mount Vernon Hospital), Hampstead from where, on 28 May, he wrote to his father:

> 'Well I am back in hospital again. I came on leave alright but I have not been feeling so rotten that I decided my leave was doing me no good, so I reported and have been sent here. I do not know what they are going to do with me as I have not seen the medical officer yet. This is a splendid hospital with an excellent situation ... What they will have me do, I do not know but I am certainly not nearly as fit as I thought I was and shall not be able to go back to France for an indefinite time... all that is really the matter with me is that I am just tired out.'[51]

This hospital was located on Hampstead Heath, and was full of quiet paths, ponds, and wildlife; the perfect place to assuage Brown's tortured psyche. It was also the hospital at which Dr Graham Anderson was posted and was able to observe enough cases to write his book. It seems at least likely that Anderson observed Brown's condition. His suffering was diagnosed as 'Stress of Service' and he was given four weeks sick leave ending on 3 July, but he actually left the left hospital on 6 June.[52] At the end of his leave he was declared fit for his instructor duties but his troubles were not over however, as at the school he suffered an almost fatal crash. On his second familiarization flight of the school's surroundings, Brown's Camel's engine cut out on takeoff and after executing a quick 180 degree turn, the aircraft tip-stalled and crashed into the ground. Stearne witnessed the crash and took a motorcycle into town to get a doctor. Roy pulled through but just barely. He recuperated at the North Riding Infirmary in Middlesbrough, then was transferred on 14 August to the 1st Northern General at Newcastle. He recovered quickly here and finally was sent to an officers' convalescent hospital nestled on the edge of the Thames. Here he wrote to his mother on 23 August 23:

> '...I do not sleep very well of course, and last night I could not sleep until four o'clock. While I was awake the nurse came in and I did not hear her till she was quite close to my bed. When I heard her I jumped and was as frightened as a baby. After that every little noise made me jump and frightened me the same. My head was pretty bad at the time. Please excuse me writing and telling you all this, I must unburden myself some time...'[53]

AERO-NEUROSIS

Obviously in addition to the severe physical trauma imparted by the crash, there were other factors at work. In a correspondence between the Air Ministry in London and the Canadian War museum it was noted by the Ministry that Roy fainted on take-off, resulting in the crash. It also mentions that the day after his fight with the Red Baron, he collapsed suffering from stomach trouble accentuated by nervous strain.[54] Bennett argues that none of these notations hold any merit, but then why would they be the official position of the Ministry? One must question efforts to depict Roy as anything more than a human being; this is the unfair and specious work of myth-builders. Brown was at the right place at the right time, but, as we now know, did not fire the fatal shot with regards to von Richtofen. His own comments suggest that he himself was unsure.

Clearly there were two sides to Brown; the outward Brown who wrote upbeat letters (as did Mannock) to family and friends, and the internal thought process and trauma that he kept to himself. He mentions to his mother that he 'must unburden myself some time' which is absolutely consistent with best practice (we now know) for mental health, and consistent with the assertions of W.H.R. Rivers as discussed earlier.

Brown was officially credited with the von Richtofen kill by the RAF, shortly after receiving a Bar to his DSC, at least partly in recognition of this feat. The citation read:

> 'Lieutenant (Honorary Captain) Arthur Roy Brown, DSC.
> 'For conspicuous gallantry and devotion to duty. On 21 April 1918, while leading a patrol of six scouts he attacked a formation of 20 hostile scouts. He personally engaged two Fokker triplanes, which he drove off; then, seeing that one of our machines was being attacked and apparently hard pressed, he dived on the hostile scout, firing all the while. This scout, a Fokker triplane, nose-dived and crashed to the ground. Since the award of the Distinguished Service Cross he has destroyed several other enemy aircraft and has shown great dash and enterprise in attacking enemy troops from low altitudes despite heavy anti-aircraft fire.'

Certainly, the RAF wanted credit for shooting down the infamous Red Baron. To give credit to those in the trenches seemed a cheat given the chivalric image that was perpetuated of the 'knights of the air' on both sides. It follows that only another pilot could possibly have shot down

Hiram Maxim sitting in front of a machine gun he made for the Sultan of Turkey in 1895. (Public domain)

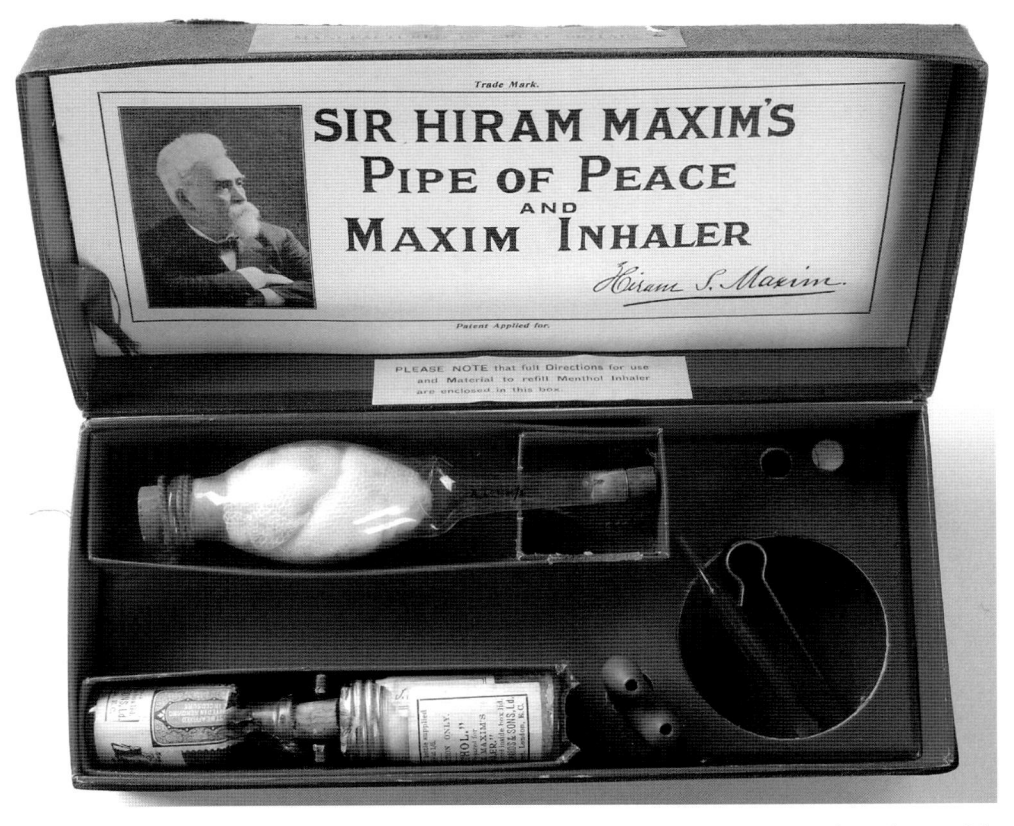

Maxim's 'Pipe of Peace' an invention for which he preferred to be remembered—not his 'killing machine' (machine gun). (Public domain)

US Marine Corps running through a gas attack in Flanders in 1917. Use of poison gas during the First World War was perhaps the most insidious of the dazzling array of new weapons available to military leadership. The choice to use it in combat has been viewed as a mistake. (NARA 165-GB-3845)

Above and opposite: Men in equipment designed to mitigate the effects of poisonous gases. Gas masks were used to neutralize chlorine gas that was in trenches and bomb craters. Also pictured is a German gas mask—masks were also fitted to dogs and horses as well as men. (NARA 165-WW-97C-1, gas mask: public domain)

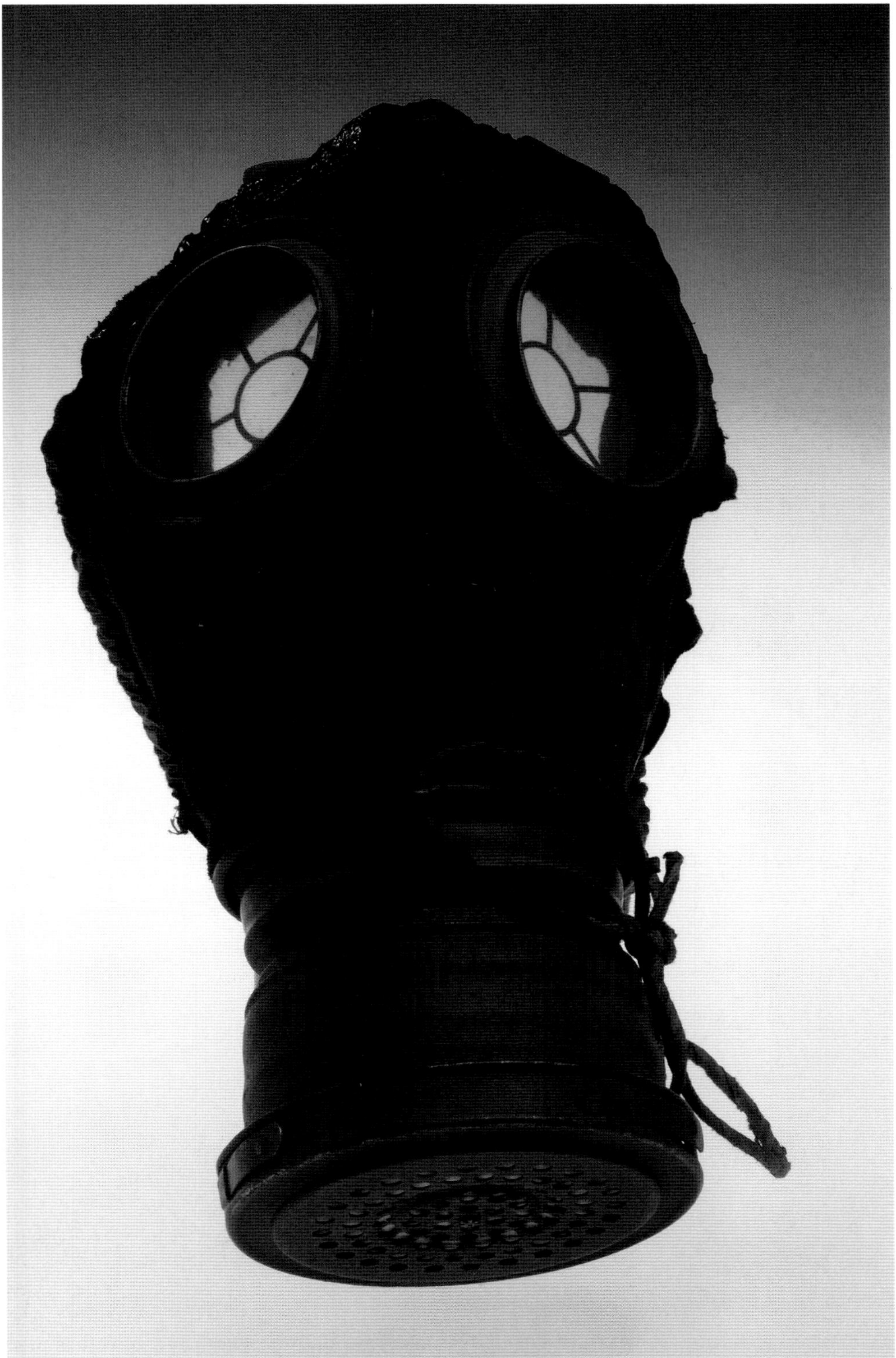

U-boat U-35 is homeward bound on the surface and is seen passing an outbound U-boat. (NARA 165-GB-3674)

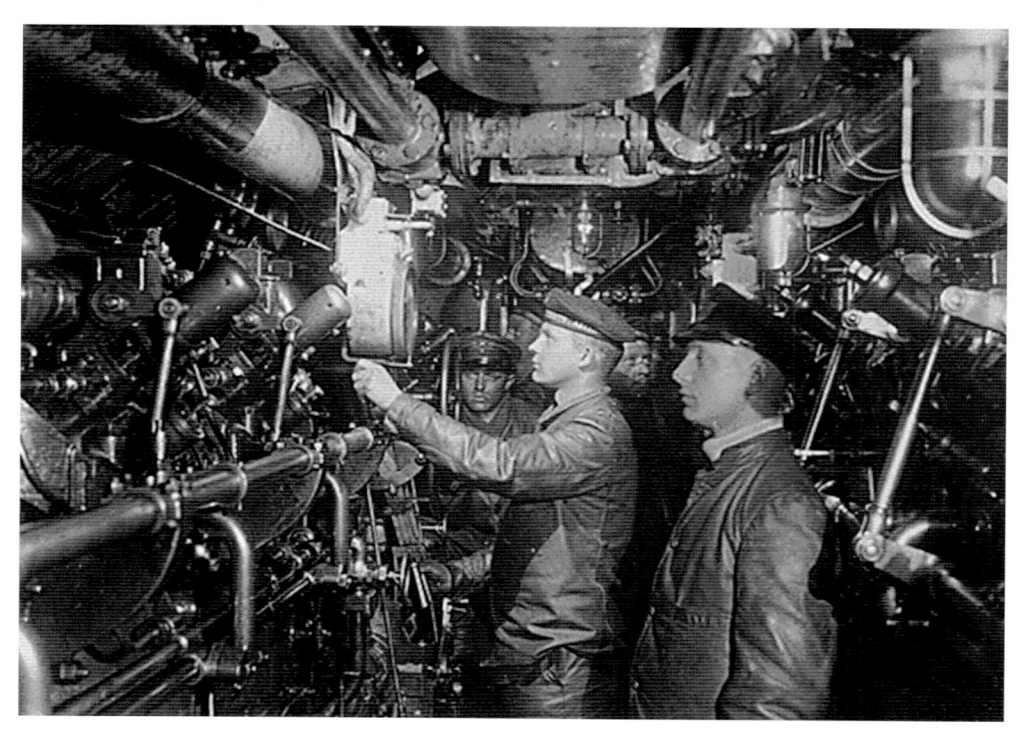

A German U-boat was crowded with gear, men, supplies, and weapons. Pictured here are the twin diesels in a U-boat's engine room. (NARA)

A huge quantity of barbed wire awaiting transport behind the Western Front in March of 1918. Barbed wire was yet another horrible invention that was used during the Great War. Originally invented to keep cattle restrained, it was quickly adapted for use in combat—many a soldier was ensnared in it then subsequently killed by machine gun or artillery fire. (NARA 165-GB-07254)

Artillery grew increasingly larger as the war progressed. Pictured here is a railway mounted cannon of huge calibre. (NARA 165-GB-6665)

The muzzle flash from a huge railway gun was both blinding and deafening. Here seen at night the fireball is especially pronounced. The devastation resulting from epic artillery shells helped give rise to the term 'brutalization' of the human body. (Public Domain)

A large quantity of captured German field artillery pieces of assorted calibres captured by the British at Amiens as part of the Battle of the Somme. (NARA)

A British Mk. V tank in the permanent collection of the Imperial War Museum in London. The tank was yet another example of faceless mechanized warfare—a war of machines which furthered de-humanized the battlefield experience of the First World War. (Public Domain)

Left: Zeppelins were slow, large, and deadly, the result of decades of balloon/airship development. The Zeppelin raids on London and Paris generated both terror and wonder. Many Parisians would watch the Zeppelin raids from rooftops and balconies at night. (Public Domain)

Below: Anthony Fokker standing in front of his Eindecker E. III—it featured a synchronized machine gun that could fire through the propeller; giving birth to the pursuit type tactics that were used for the rest of the war and all subsequent wars. (Photo courtesy of Achim Engels)

Pictured are SE. 5as and Fokker Dr. 1 triplanes engaged in a dogfight. Tactics in aerial combat evolved swiftly during the Great War; here the quintessential 'turn fighter'—the Dr. 1 is pitted against part of the next generation of fighter that employed diving at high speed on its prey and then climbing back up to altitude. (Creative Commons)

Base or 'stationary' hospitals sprung up like mushrooms across the Western Front, France, and England to cope with the unparalleled casualties of the War. This hospital was located at St. Pol, France and supported the Arras and Cambrai campaign. (NARA 165-BO-1766)

These German soldiers suffered minor wounds and are seen amusing themselves. Physical wounds were relatively straightforward to treat; the psychological trauma experienced by combatants was not. (NARA 165-GB-03551)

The Craiglockhart hydropathic hospital became a treatment center for soldiers suffering from psychological traumas such as 'shell shock' and other nervous disorders. (Public Domain)

W.H. Rivers, a doctor whose theories concerning psychological trauma focused on patients confronting and talking about their suffering as a means to heal. River's theories were groundbreaking for the time but presaged modern treatment methods. (Public Domain)

Lt. Elliott White Springs in flying gear in front of his Sopwith Camel on September 9, 1918. Springs was a member of the 148th American Aero Squadron. (NARA)

Left: The 'Three Musketeers' John Grider, Larry Callahan, and E.W. Springs—who is standing on the far right. (Courtesy of the Springs Close Family Archives)

Below: Lt. Springs, commander of 'B' Flight is third from left, on his right is Larry Callahan. The pilots are standing in front of a Camel of the 148th American Squadron. (NARA)

William C. Lambert writing a letter home in a moment of repose. Lambert's combat fatigue descended upon him by surprise; his subconscious suffering finally punching through to his conscious mind and incapacitating him. (Public Domain)

Capt. Roy Brown, who checked into a hospital for nervous exhaustion several days after seeing the body of the 'Red Baron' – a man he was originally credited with killing. (Public Domain)

Maj. Edward 'Mick' Mannock in flying gear near the tail of an SE 5a. (Image courtesy of Greg VanWyngarden)

Mannock was a sensitive and pensive individual who loved animals; today this would be a textbook description of someone who should not be a fighter pilot. Here he is pictured with a canine friend. (Image courtesy of Greg VanWyngarden)

Right: Ernst Udet is seen in this posed photograph early in his career. Images such as these helped galvanize the profile of the 'immortal ace' in the public eye. (Public Domain)

Below: Udet in a Siemens Schukert D. III. (Image courtesy Greg VanWyngarden)

George Guynemer—the unlikely ace—standing next to Capitaine Brocard. Guynemer's fiery spirit was contained within a slight frame, and was famous for his saying: 'Unless one has given all, one has given nothing'. (Public Domain)

Guynemer's Spad VII *Vieux Charles*—a name he bestowed on all of his aircraft. Guynemer is in the cockpit in this image by Robert Soubiran—a member of the Lafayette Escadrille. (NARA)

BESTING THE BARON – ROY BROWN

Germany's finest ace. Even the text of his citation remains carefully neutral in ascribing credit to Brown for shooting down von Richthofen; it describes what happened without drawing conclusions, although it does imply that Brown was a good marksman.

In 1919, Brown left the RAF and returned to Canada where he worked as an accountant for a time, but eventually aviation reasserted itself. In 1928, he founded a small airline, General Airways Limited, and worked for a while as editor of *Canadian Aviation*. When the Second World War erupted, he tried to enlist in the Royal Canadian Air Force but was refused. He instead entered politics, losing an election for the Ontario legislature in 1943. He later purchased a farm near Stouffville, Ontario. He died on 9 March 1944, of a heart attack at the age of 50, at his farm in Stouffville, shortly after posing for a photograph with a Canadian flying ace, George Beurling. He is buried, with his wife, Edythe, in the Toronto Necropolis. Brown was inducted into the Canadian Aviation Hall of Fame in 2015.

Chapter 10

The Conscience of a Hawk – Ernst Udet

Ernst Udet was son of an engineer, born in Frankfurt but raised in Munich, a name given to the city due to the Benedictine monks whose monastery was nestled in the Old Town areas. During the first decade of the twentieth century, Munich saw continued growth economically and culturally. Thomas Mann wrote somewhat ironically in his novella *Gladius Dei* about this period: 'München leuchtete' (literally 'Munich shone'). Munich was a city of beer, with the annual Oktoberfest in the city centre, and numerous breweries called this city home which fuelled the numerous Biergartens that dotted the city and were a favourite place to hang out. If one had a light breakfast and needed a snack, a plate of white sausage (Münchner Weißwurst), spicy sweet mustard and soft pretzel, perhaps from the Viktualienmarkt, Munich's most popular market for fresh food and delicatessen, would have hit the spot. Of all the towns in which the fliers in this book grew up, Munich was the most cosmopolitan and urbane, a very large and densely populated city.

This was the bustling environment where young Udet cultivated a fascination for the early aviators, the Wrights, Bleriot, Curtiss, and others. In 1909, the same year that Bleriot flew the Channel and the Grande Semaine d'Aviation took place at Rheims, he joined a local model aircraft club. At the outbreak of the war in 1914, under-aged Udet volunteered. In 1915, he funded his own training course at the Otto School of Flying in Munich to become a pilot so that he could join the fledgling German Air Service. His first months proved disastrous and, following a crash, he experienced a brief nervous breakdown,[1] testimony that this was a sensitive and thoughtful young man. If one subscribes to the Beard school of thought, given the context of his upbringing Udet may have been mildly neurasthenic before even learning to fly. That being said, the urban context in which he grew up would be an asset in the coming years as '…urban men were ideal [psychologically] because they were "less perturbed by the noise of modern battle"'.[2]

THE CONSCIENCE OF A HAWK – ERNST UDET

After training with the Air Reserve Group, he was finally accepted by the German Air Service as a pilot for Lieutenant Justinus of 206 squadron during the summer of 1915, flying the Aviatik B two-seater.[3] Lance Corporal Udet was then transferred to single seat fighters at Habsheim,[4] where he would fly the new Fokker Eindecker E.III. The following is an account of his first encounter with a French Caudron:

> 'Very soon he was so close that I could see the observer's head. With his rectangular goggles he resembled some great, ferocious insect bent upon my destruction. The moment had now come for me to shoot in earnest – but I was quite unable to do so! It was as though horror had turned my blood to ice, taken the strength from my arms, and numbed my brain. I sat passively in the cockpit, flying straight ahead, and staring idiotically at the Caudron as we passed each other. Suddenly the Caudron's machine gun opened fire; there were sharp metallic sounds as the bullets struck my Fokker, the machine gave a shudder, and I felt a hard blow which smashed my goggles. Mechanically I reached to my face to feel the splintered glass, and when I withdrew my hand it was covered in blood. I pushed the stick forward, and nose-dived into the clouds. My mind was in a whirl. What happened, what was the reason for my strange conduct? "you miserable coward!" the engine seemed to say. And my only thought was "thank god, nobody saw it!"'[5]

In this passage, Udet shows himself to be an imaginative man, comparing the enemy aviator to 'some great, ferocious insect bent upon my destruction'. If there is one commonality with all the medical tracts from the Great War, it is the agreement that imagination is no asset to the combat aviators' psyche. Udet was, no doubt, a bit anxious this being his first patrol in a new fighter – the Fokker E. III – a plane that featured wing warping for roll, and a full flying horizontal stabilizer and rudder. Modern audiences should remember that flying these early planes was an art in itself. Andrew Carter of The Australian Vintage Aviation Society had this to say about flying his museum's E.III replica:

> 'The early Gnome rotary engine is one of the simplest types. It has a single fuel lever, to control the amount of fuel going into the crankcase, but [with] no throttle it runs at full power

or nothing… I "blip" the engine to as slow as possible and the chocks are removed. Blipping is using a button on the control column that, when pressed and held in, stops all sparking and kills the engine momentarily. This is the limited power control these early engines had. I release the button, the engine goes to full power and I am off. There is no feedback through the control column or rudder pedals. You simply ease forward on the column, enough to get the skid off the ground and apply small rudder pressure to keep straight. You have to use visual clues as you don't feel anything through the controls. In a very short distance (less than sixty feet) the aircraft breaks ground and climbs straight ahead. It is a stable aircraft with a powerful engine. The full flying stabilator is ridiculously, overly, sensitive, in fact at times, it is downright scary! The Eindecker was fitted with a simple friction control lever at the base of the control column to overcome this control sensitivity. The well balanced rudder without a fixed fin is also incredibly effective. Wing warping, as expected, does work but is not the most effective form of roll control. There is a fair amount of effort required (I have to use two hands on the stick) for a sluggish result. However, combined with rudder, balanced turns are easy to do and co-ordinate. It has been written that some pilots found turning right through 270 degrees was quicker than turning ninety degrees left! This is due to the gyroscopic effect of rotary engines, turns to the left are slower, and make the nose of the aircraft rise, and turns to the right, are quick but tended to pull the nose down. The high drag E.III cruises slowly (less than sixty knots), despite the 100 horsepower up front. To ensure smooth engine operation you need to keep the pressure in the fuel tank fairly constant, at about one psi. Reports I had read stated this may mean pumping eight or more times per hour. So, understandably, the pressure gauge is the largest instrument in the cockpit, although a change in note of the engine is the best indication that the pressure is low and needs attention. You have to be careful not to over-pressurise it as this can cause a rich mixture which is equally as detrimental as a lean one. The real challenge will be in moving fuel from the rear tank to the front tank and still keeping pressure to the

THE CONSCIENCE OF A HAWK – ERNST UDET

engine constant. This is something I haven't attempted yet, and will spend a lot of time doing it on the ground before I try it in flight. Like all good things, the flight comes to an end far too soon and I have to start descending. I tend to start blipping before I turn base. I hold the button in for quite a few seconds at a time before releasing it just for a second at a time. This "more off than on" technique allows me to ease forward and descend quite comfortably. However, anytime I need to steepen the angle of bank or exit the turn, I have to let off the button to get a burst of slipstream over the rudder and elevator which instantly energizes their effectiveness. It glides very well (although steeply). I tend to keep high and slightly fast and come in steep in case the engine fails altogether. I keep blipping the engine all the way into the flare. I simply transition through the flare, letting off the blip switch momentarily every few seconds, and a smooth landing is assured. The British test report of a captured E.III stated it would be very tiring to fly in anything but the smoothest conditions. I agree with this completely.'[6]

The previous description pertains to more or less level flight and gentle manoeuvres. Now imagine this machine in combat! It is hard to envisage aces like Max Immelmann inventing his namesake turn in such an aircraft, but he did.[7] Udet had to learn this new machine, plus for the first time he was alone and facing an enemy. When he finally returned to his aerodrome, he tortured himself over what had happened:

'...I then went to my room, and threw myself on the bed. I wanted to sleep, but my thoughts refused to let me rest. "is one a coward just because one fails in ones very first fight?" I tried to reassure myself; told myself that it was just a matter of nerves – a thing that might happen to anyone. But my conscience was not to be easily appeased, and there remained the cold, hard fact that I had failed miserably, and all because, at the crucial moment, I had thought of myself, and had trembled for my own safety...there and then I vowed to make myself a "good soldier" I would shoot better and fly better, until I was in a position to rid myself of the stain that now lay upon my honour.'[8]

AERO-NEUROSIS

One could argue that Udet was far too hard on himself. But at the time, honour, Prussianism, and notions of manhood conspired to compound his suffering. Udet expected himself to behave as dispassionately as the machine he was flying. This idea that flyers must possess sang froid, precision, a calculating sense, is recurrent in the literature not only of the First World War but today as well. Training programmes in modern air forces do much to cultivate this sensibility but in 1914, combat flying had not even been invented yet! Combat flying evolved in real time in a high-stakes experimental fashion; if it worked a new manoeuvre was born; if not, the pilot usually perished. The following passage Udet recounts a seminal moment in his career as a fighter pilot:

> 'The moment had come. My heart beat furiously, and the hands which held the joy-stick were damp. It was one against twenty-three! My Fokker flew above the enemy squadron like a hawk singling out its victim. The hawk followed, but did not pounce. But even as I hesitated, I realized that if I failed to open the battle immediately I should never have the courage to do so afterwards. In that case I would land, go to my room, and then, in the morning, Pfalzer would have the task of writing my father that there had been a fatal accident while I was cleaning my revolver.'[9]

It is interesting how, even this early, Udet thought of suicide as a 'way out' from his plight which would replay its final iteration during the Second World War with Hermann Göring, one of those with whom he bonded during this defining period and to whom he had a lasting allegiance. Göring ultimately betrayed Udet or so Udet thought resulting in a burden he could not stand. The following passage illustrates Udet's attempt at compartmentalizing his thought processes regarding the fact that he was killing human beings:

> 'At the time the thought that those men were human beings never once occurred to me; I was only conscious of one sensation – victory, triumph! The iron band about my chest snapped, and the blood coursed freely through my veins – the tension was over, I had been blooded.'[10]

It is important to remember that Udet wrote his memoirs many years after the image of the ace had been established by press and others. He may have crafted his story to fit into these global archetypes of the quintessential ace. Also, the now well-documented 'blood lust'[11] may have become manifest which would explain his feeling of release and being 'blooded'. The following statement is further evidence of the fact that his tract was written at a wiser age, as it seems almost apologetic in tone: 'We were young, and victory had to be celebrated'.[12] This statement undergirds the sobering fact that all wars are fought mainly by young men; as if they were older and wiser, they might not be fought at all.

Lieutenant Heinrich Gontermann was Udet's new *Staffelfuhrer* or squadron leader, a man who had already shot down twelve planes and six balloons. Udet wrote that 'his tactics were completely new to us. Before opening fire against an opponent, he endeavoured to force him down by superior flying'.[13] Another notion of the initial reluctance of many aviators to open fire on other aircraft, a phenomenon that would disappear forever by the end of the war. Udet clearly admired Gontermann who clearly did show mercy to his victims:

'On 24 March, I shot down a Sopwith two-seater during a Geschwader fight over our lines. I attacked him from close behind right at the start of the Geschwader fight, after which he immediately went down so that I had him alone. I always stayed on his tail but only shot whenever he made a move to break away. I had fired 60 shots from about 20 to 30 meters distance and was surprised that he landed safely and that both occupants were unharmed.[14]

'On the 13th, we encountered an English squadron over our lines. During the course of the Geschwader battle, I forced the leader of the Englishmen – who was identified by two streamers – into a dogfight. Most of the time, I stayed on his tail and shot at him. He flew quite skilfully and turned incredibly fast, but didn't get a chance to shoot. After about three minutes, the pilot appeared to have been wounded. The machine descended in large, regular turns. I stayed behind him but didn't shoot anymore. I hoped he would land safely. But at about 1,000 meters altitude, the machine turned over and plunged vertically, somersaulting, into the earth. I went there in a car. Both occupants were dead. One is always very sorry about that, but I could not have done anything else. He defended himself too well.

AERO-NEUROSIS

The unfortunate crewmen were Capt. L.S. Platt (pilot) and 2Lt. T. Margerison, who crashed between Vitry-en-Artois and Brebieres.'[15]

Seemingly, Gontermann would only fire if necessary, preferring to threaten opponents on the ground, as many of his victims landed safely and became prisoners of war. Udet continues his description of Gontermann:

> 'He had unlimited faith in himself. But there was one thing about him which caused me to wonder. If, when he landed, bullet-holes were found on his machine, he was intensely annoyed. He regarded them as proof that there had been something wrong with his flying. He argued that if you conducted your campaign in the right manner your opponent should never get the chance of a shot at you.'[16]

Gontermann seems to have been at the very least a mild control freak, or perhaps it was simply a unique mental construct that insured that if he flew well enough he would never get hit, removing the element of chance and the 'fog of war' and returning control to himself. Given the complexities of aerial combat his approach seems unsustainable at best, and rather the exception than the rule. Udet continued by stating that 'In contrast to the Red Baron – if his mechanics reported hits on his machine, he would simply shrug his shoulders and forget about them'.[17] Gontermann's successes had earned him the *Pour le Merite* decoration (the Blue Max) for which he was also granted a leave. Udet was placed in charge of the squadron during his absence. He describes this period as busy, flying three times a day or more. On 25 May, his flight met up with one of France's greatest aces:

> 'I am not prepared to swear that there is such a thing as a sixth sense, but certainly on that flight I had a sudden feeling that all was not well, that some hidden danger threatened us. I made a half-turn, and a moment later I saw Puz's machine enveloped in smoke and flames. Puz was sitting perfectly still, his body stiffly erect in the cockpit, his face turned towards me. He slowly raised an arm to his helmet. It might have been a last struggle, but it looked exactly as though he were saluting me for the last time.
>
> "'Puz!" I shouted, "Puz!" But in that instant his machine broke up, the engine dropped like a flaming meteor, and the broken

THE CONSCIENCE OF A HAWK – ERNST UDET

wings fluttered after it. For several moments I was incapable of thought. I simply stared overboard at the fallen wreckage. A hostile plane hove into sight, about fifteen hundred feet below me flying at high speed towards the west. The red white and blue cockades seemed to stare up at me like vicious eyes. Immediately something told me: that can only be Guynemer.'[18]

Clearly Udet was deeply disturbed by the lightning fast and accurate attack by Guynemer and again he attributes anthropomorphic qualities to the cockades of Guynemer's Spad staring at him like 'vicious eyes'. Also, the superstitious feeling that all was not well; intuition or a chance coalescing of factors. Or it could be that, writing years later, Udet wished to attach a special significance to the battle, further burnishing the notion of Guynemer as France's ace of aces. After they landed, Udet noticed Corporal Willy Glinkermann, another pilot in the flight that day, was also deeply disturbed by the savage attack:

'Glinkermann stood a little apart from the rest, immersed in thought, and scribbling designs in the sand with the point of his walking stick. His dog was beside him, rubbing his nose against his master's knee. But Glinkermann was beyond taking notice of the animal; his thoughts were elsewhere. As I approached him he lifted his head and looked at me.

"You mustn't blame me, Knagges," he said. "I really couldn't prevent it. He came down at us straight out of the sun, and by the time I realized what was happening it was all over." Pain had distorted his features. I knew him, and realized that he would torture himself with reproaches and doubts for weeks to come. Having flown in line with Puz, he would keep telling himself that he ought to have prevented his death.'[19]

In the next day or so, Glinkermann would fall just as Puz Hanisch had. Udet noted that 'Glinkermann had not come back…he had disappeared in the clouds and was last seen flying towards the west. The old story, the old, bitter story…'[20] Udet described a poignant image of all that remained of Glinkermann:

'On the flying field, plunged into the soft turf, stood a walking stick. A military peaked cap hung from the handle. Glinkermann's talisman. When he started out on a flight he left them there; and on his return he took them away with him. A big, wolf-like Alsatian wandered restlessly up and down near the stick. As I walked over the field, he trotted to meet me. He never did that at other times. He was essentially a one-man dog, and growled fiercely at anyone who came near Glinkermann. Now he buried his cold, damp nose affectionately in my hand. I had the greatest difficulty in concealing the despair which I felt.'[21]

In contrast to the unspoken axiom that pilots shouldn't obsess over dead comrades, Udet was clearly disturbed by the loss of Glinkermann:

'Night came slowly. I sat by the open window, and stared into the gathering darkness. A new moon rose from behind the big trees in the park. The noise of crickets was unusually loud and unbearably irritating. The atmosphere was sultry: there would be rain before morning. I had Glinkermann's dog in my room. The wretched animal could not settle down, but walked continually backwards and forwards to the door. Occasionally, he howled dismally. Glinkermann, Glinkermann! A week before he had brought down a Spad that was about to dive on my tail...he had to come back! I could not be left alone!'[22]

Udet wrote with a heavy heart that he was the last survivor of the original group of pilots that comprised Jasta 15. It seemed his own mortality might be a distinct possibility. Soon he was to meet up with Puz's killer, the slight French ace with the burning black eyes, Georges Guynemer, in an epic duel that left a lasting impression with Udet, and importantly, underscored the notion that chivalry in the skies was not dead. This must have come as a shot in the arm for Udet who was clearly suffering from the mounting losses of his friends and comrades in arms:

'Then, from the west, a small object rapidly approached. Small and black at first, it quickly grew in size and soon I recognized it as a Spad...I braced myself in my cockpit, for I knew there was going to be a fight...soon we were circling round each other, playing for an opening...sometimes we passed so near to each other that I could see every detail of my opponent's face...on the machine's side there was a stork and two words painted in white. The fifth time that

THE CONSCIENCE OF A HAWK – ERNST UDET

he flew past me—so close that I could feel the draught of his propeller—I managed to spell out a word: "V-i-e-u-x". And *Vieux Charles* was Guynemer's insignia… I threw a half-loop, with the object of getting at him from above, but immediately he grasped my purpose and half rolled out of the way. I tried another maneuver, but again Guynemer forestalled me and the jockeying for position continued. Once, as I was coming out of a turn, he had the advantage of me for a few seconds, and a regular hailstorm of bullets rattled against my wings. I tried every trick I knew—turns, loops, rolls, and side-slips—but he followed each movement with lightning speed and gradually I began to realize that he was more than a match for me…I went into a steep turn, and for a moment I had him at the end of my sights. I pressed the trigger…there was no response … my gun had jammed! We still flew in circles round each other. It was a wonderful flying experience – if one could forget that one's life was at stake. I have never had to deal with a more skilful opponent, and for a while I completely forgot that he was Guynemer, my enemy. It seemed to me, rather, that I was having some practice over the aerodrome with an old friend…for eight minutes we had been flying round each other in circles, and they were the longest eight minutes that I have ever experienced. Suddenly Guynemer looped, and flew on his back over my head. At that moment I relinquished hold of the stick, and hammered with both hand at the machine gun…Guynemer had observed my actions and now knew that I was his helpless victim. He again passed close over my head, flying almost on his back, And then, to my great surprise, he raised his arm and waved to me. Immediately afterwards he dived away towards the west, in the direction of his own lines. I flew home stupefied…I believe that Guynemer gave proof that even in modern warfare there is still something left of the knightly chivalry of bygone days. And accordingly, I lay this belated wreath on Guynemer's unknown grave.'[23]

Udet was in command of Jagdstaffel 37 when the commander Grashoff was transferred to Macedonia. Shortly thereafter, Baron Manfred von Richthofen asked him to join Jasta 11; Udet quickly agreed.[24] Von Richthofen was led

Jasta 11 but also under his command were Jastas 4,6 and 10.[25] After joining the Red Baron's flying circus, Udet was given his first opportunity to fly the famous Fokker Dr. 1 triplane.

If Udet was struggling with his emotions regarding combat flying, von Richthofen was the perfect antidote to whatever doubts he may have had. For the Baron, killing was a profession and he did it extremely well, actually taking pleasure in strafing runs of troop columns on the ground, in strident contrast to Springs, Lambert and Mannock. Udet described him as:

> 'the simplest man I ever met. He was a Prussian through and through. A great soldier. Eating, drinking and sleeping were all that he granted life, and then only the minimum that was necessary to keep flesh and blood in working order.'[26]

Von Richthofen took good care of the pilots in his Jastas and he especially liked Udet, giving him command of Jasta 11 soon after he joined. It was not due to emotionalism but instead for 'purely material reasons…his whole life was dedicated to an ideal, the ideal of country, and he demanded the same service from his pilots'.[27] So von Richthofen liked those who shared his ideology and would help further his goal of destroying the enemy in the service of the fatherland. Udet continues 'once you had proved your worth, he supported you by every means in his power…if you were a failure, he dropped you without a second's hesitation, without the flicker of an eyelid. A single mistake…and he had to leave the squadron—on the same day.'[28]

Von Richthofen may have been as mercenary as Udet describes, but for those who measured up he took very good care of them:

> 'When food supplies grew difficult to obtain, he used to dispatch Bodenschatz, a prince among adjutants, in an old plane with orders to see what he could scrounge at the base, Bodenschatz on these occasions took with him a large number of photographs bearing Richthofen's own signature. In the quartermaster stores at the base these pictures were highly valued, with the result that the squadron never went short of sausage and ham.'[29]

Posed studio portraits of aces helped craft the image of their larger than life status among troops on the ground; they were regarded as celebrities like modern day movie or rock stars, as this passage clearly illustrates.

THE CONSCIENCE OF A HAWK – ERNST UDET

The iconic hand-signed images of the Baron, with his cold, clear eyes with the slightly drooping eyelids, seemed to exude German strength and resolve and acted as currency when times were tough. Udet clearly admired the Baron, as did some allied pilots, but many had a different view of his tactics and style such as Arthur Gould Lee:

> '[he] was no Superman, and by no means a super pilot. He was brave but he was wary, seldom entering into a free-for-all dogfight, where chance played as important a role as skill, but waiting "on the fringe" for stragglers. Then he would pounce. When he did take part in close in fighting, usually had wingman to protect his tail. But the acknowledged ascendancy he had acquired, so cleverly exploited by the German propaganda organization, gave him an immeasurable prestige, which even then was becoming a mystique, and yet he was worthy of it, for he was a natural fighter and leader and a stranger to fear, at least until he was wounded.'[30]

Lee notes that even the Baron underwent a change after he was wounded, becoming more careful, more protective of his men, and realizing that he too, may one day soon fall. Mick Mannock had a far darker view of the Baron as we shall see in the following chapter.

Udet took off with Siegfried Gussmann on 28 March 1918, to patrol above Albert. Udet's wingman was attacked, and while this was occurring, Udet was attacked by another plane at roughly the same altitude; both exchanged bursts from three separate head-on passes. On the fourth pass, Udet began to feel the pressure of the duel:

> 'I felt my hands grow damp. Opposing me was a man fighting the battle of his life. It was either he or I – only one of us would be left – there was no alternative.'[31]

Udet scored the lethal burst on the fifth and final pass causing the British plane to half roll and dived, finally impacting in a shell crater. Udet circled over the wreck contemplating what had happened and catching his breath. He described the aftermath:

> 'I flew back to the aerodrome, my skin soaked in perspiration, and my nerves in a desperately excited state. At the same time,

I felt a dull, persistent pain my ears. I had made it a rule never to let myself worry about the men I shot down. He who fights should not look at the wounds he inflicts. But, on this particular occasion, I felt an insatiable desire to know who my opponent had been. Towards evening, in the dusk, I made my way to the scene of the crash…my opponent…had been shot through the head…the doctor handed me his wallet… "Lieutenant C.R. Massdorp, Ontario, RFC 47". Also in the wallet were a picture of an elderly woman and a letter. It said: "don't be too reckless. Think of father and me" … I drove back to my unit. Somehow one had to try to get rid of the thought that a mother wept for every man one shot down.'[32]

Udet was obviously a sensitive man; in spite of monolithic warrior rhetoric as we have seen with Brown, (it was he or I, one must do one's duty, etc.) he could not escape his humanity. The pain in his ear became steadily worse, probably the result of high altitude flying or rapid descents from higher to lower altitudes, so von Richthofen ordered Udet to take a leave to recuperate. The following morning the Baron saw Udet off in a two-seater. As he took off, von Richthofen waved with his cap; Udet noted that 'his fair hair shone in the sun'. It was the last time Udet saw him alive.

Udet returned to Munich in the early morning by train. Even though he had come home, Udet sensed something had changed; that which was familiar suddenly and unexpectedly felt strange. Upon visiting Udet's family doctor, he was told his flying days were over, which hit him hard. He returned with his father to the family home for a meal:

'We sat down to lunch. From time to time they questioned me, and I related only what I thought was good for them. I said nothing about my last duel, the one with Massdorp. I did not want to alarm my father; and, furthermore, it was something about which I felt some reluctance to speak. And, in any case, over Sauerbraten and Klossen, I could not speak of a man whose death I had caused, a man whose bravery had won my respect.'[33]

Like British squadrons, it was considered counter-productive in German Jastas to mention news or events that would erode morale, which is why Udet did not mention his encounter with Massdorp to his fellow pilots.

THE CONSCIENCE OF A HAWK – ERNST UDET

After a few days of much needed rest, Udet was able to ascertain his new 'home' and it was not in Munich:

> 'Well I was home…I seldom went into the city. What was there for me to do there? My friends were at the front, many of them had been killed, and I felt no particular desire to mix with strangers.'[34]

This theme is common among First World War soldiers and flyers. In Remarque's *All Quiet*, Paul shares a similar sentiment about the binary view of the Front versus home-life. When Udet met his childhood sweetheart, Eleanor Lo Zinck, he was brusque, frank and to the point; alarmingly so. 'Lo ', Udet's nickname for his girlfriend, was still adherent to social conventions of peacetime but Udet, espousing a *carpe diem* ethos learned at the Front, suggested that:

> '"We should be absolutely free from all restrictions, and could live as freely as though we were on another planet." At first she laughed, then her lips grew tight. "But that's impossible…what would my parents have to say?" "I'm sorry," I said. "I'm afraid being at the front has made me forget the conventions. You mustn't be angry…" I shrugged my shoulders. "Angry? Of course not." And yet I had a feeling that something was wrong. We had become different men since being at the front. Things which we had formerly considered important now seemed of no account. Other things filled our life. Without being able to express it in words, I had a sudden feeling that I wanted to rejoin my comrades at the front.'[35]

Again, we see the notion that these men were forever changed, transformed into something that only made sense at the front. While on leave, Udet received news of von Richthofen's death which 'affected him profoundly'. He longed to return to the front even more, harassing his doctor to pass him as fit to fly again. Even when he was with Lo his thoughts drifted back to combat flying:

> 'And yet…there were times, when we were lying side by side on the grass, staring into the sky, when I caught myself searching the cumulus clouds which gathered above us. Would

AERO-NEUROSIS

a machine suddenly dive out of them? And in the mornings, when I got up, my first act was to look at the sky. What sort of flying weather were we having?'[36]

Able to bear the subterfuge no longer, Udet finally confessed to Lo that 'there are times when I wish I were back at the front',[37] such was the bond to the men and life at the front that had supplanted any semblance of a normal life. Lo did not take this well and mistook Udet's meaning to be a lack of affection for her, when in fact he spoke of the unique bond formed by soldiers and pilots who share the crucible of combat. Udet commented that his mother would have understood as his father was a soldier.

The war was slowly winding down; It was 22 August 1918, the height of summer and a very warm day. To those in leaderships positions, victory no longer seemed certain for Germany. Udet recounts being chased by a flight of three S.E.5s after he shot down their flight leader. Two peeled off and returned to their lines but one intensified the pursuit so that he was no more than 100 feet behind Udet's Fokker D. VII. Udet recounted that 'a bullet had exploded and set fire to the tracer ammunition'. Udet was always cool and collected in his thinking and this is what saved him; he fired his guns thereby expelling the smouldering ammunition into the air, the smoke from which resembled an aircraft on fire, causing his pursuer to break off the attack.[38] This encounter rattled Udet to such an extent that:

> 'When I landed, I remained for some time seated in the cockpit. Berend had to help me out of the machine. I went to the squadron office. "Göring arrives this evening," said the orderly-room sergeant. I looked at him with vacant eyes. "Hauptmann Göring, our new squadron leader," he repeated. "Oh indeed," my voice sounded strange and toneless. I wanted to get leave. At once. That very moment. I didn't want our new leader to see me in my present state of nerves.'[39]

Udet took a leave after this incident such was his state of nervous exhaustion. When he returned he acheived his 62nd and final victory, before his fuel tank and thigh were hit by an enemy bullet causing him to land. The end of the war came as a strange relief for Udet, even though he outwardly was glad, his transformation was complete as someone who had become a creature of the war context – he no longer felt at home doing anything else. He relates how he and fellow fliers would gather for a beer after the war:

THE CONSCIENCE OF A HAWK – ERNST UDET

'In the evening we ex-airmen often used to gather in a little Brauhausstube. We were in a depressed mood. They had thrown us out, and few of us had the remotest idea how we were going to settle down in civilian life. "you know" said Greim to me, one day, "if only we could fly again, and take a look at all this mess from above, it wouldn't be so bad." We sipped at our drinks, and stared straight ahead.'[40]

After the war, Udet became an exhibition pilot and air racer, worked for Hollywood, married and divorced Lo Zinck in the span of three years, and started an unsuccessful aircraft company. None of these pursuits seemed to fill the void created by the end of the war. However, Udet felt by flying he would be continuing in some capacity to further the influence of aviation. He was to serve again in the Second World War under his old squadron commander, Herman Göring, for which he was grateful as he felt 'we were soldiers without a flag. We had now unfurled our flag once more. The Fuhrer restored it to us. For old soldiers, life is again worth living'.[41] However, Udet's role was largely administrative, the bureaucracy of which drove him to drink excessively. He was a strong proponent of the dive bomber and was responsible for the development and eventual production of the Stuka Ju 87. None of this measured up to combat, and perhaps he realized that for him, air combat was firmly fixed in the past. Udet took his own life in 1942 when he felt Göring had betrayed him, writing on the wall: 'Ingelein [his girlfriend, Inge Bleyle], why have you left me?' and 'Iron One [Hermann Göring], you are responsible for my death.'[42]

Chapter 11

Edward 'Mick' Mannock – Collectivist Dogfighter

Edward 'Mick' Mannock was born in 1889 and came from working class Irish stock but was raised in rural England and India. His family consisted of his 'mother, father and three other siblings. His father was not suited for family life and resented the obligations of fatherhood, often taking this out on the children. As a result, Mick 'became a silent child, devoted to reading and studying animals and birds'.[1] His father was a soldier in the 5th Dragoon Guards and was posted to India to serve in the garrison at Meerut. His mother, Julia, tried her best to serve as firewall to the father's foul temper which made Mick withdraw even further, internalizing the turmoil and perhaps creating a silent longing for a sense of a happy family that he would eventually get with his squadron. He was of slight frame and pensive 'with such depths as to baffle the comprehension of adults'.[2] He had a bad eye from an early age, but it looked normal.[3]

On the troopship returning from India, he seldom played with the other children. Noticing this, Julia attempted to draw him out. Her kindly tricks did not work. It seemed to her that the boy was old before his time. He did not get on very well with anybody…and had no real opinions about anything.[4] Mick had a great liking for music. He had his own violin, acquired by his father in India. His only other possessions were books. He seemed lost in himself.[5] As a young man he was 'renowned for his ability to daydream for long periods'[6], something that would bear bitter fruit when he became a fighter pilot.

They settled in a house in Canterbury. The inner city was a network of cramped streets, small shops and compact housing which for nearly ten years Mannock called home.[7] Adrian Smith wrote that:

> 'For soldiers and civilians alike, Edwardian Canterbury was "all parsons and pubs"—on the one hand England's premier

EDWARD 'MICK' MANNOCK – COLLECTIVIST DOGFIGHTER

cathedral city, and on the other a modest-sized market town in east Kent surrounded by hop fields and orchards...what was remarkable about Canterbury was how little it had changed since Dickens's day.'[8]

Julia moved the family to 'Jones cottages' and every Sunday the family would have walked through Northgate, and around the city wall, in order to attend Mass at St. Thomas of Canterbury Roman Catholic Church. [9] Dad returned then left for good. Twenty years later he showed up at Buckingham Palace to claim Mick's posthumous Victoria Cross.[10]

After he left, the two sons and two daughters were practically destitute. He had been improvident for years and there was not a penny to spare. In those days poverty meant real privation. Julia's Irish pride prevented her from asking for help from friends. Young Edward saw the symbols of poverty all around him; the patched clothes, mother's habit of counting half-pennies and her efforts at cooking the cheapest foods for maximum nourishment.[11]

It was time for Edward to get a job to help his family – his brother Patrick was already a clerk – so Edward worked for a greengrocer, blistering his hands from hefting sacks of vegetables.[12] Next, he worked for a barber, then begrudgingly took a clerking job at the National Telephone company in Canterbury. He found clerking stifling and dull, so he became a telephone linesman where he could at least work outside, which prompted his move to Wellingborough, Northamptonshire.[13]

He met Jim Eyles at this time, who became a second father to Edward, filling a void that had existed since early childhood. Eyles got him better lodgings, and it was thanks to Eyles that we have information on how profoundly Mick suffered.

Young Mannock was becoming an extreme socialist with an admiration for James Keir Hardie.[14] Mannock found much common ground with Hardie; both men grew up in poor surroundings without their biological father, both were used to a life of toil, Hardie founded the Independent Labour party and became its first leader, later being elected to Parliament. For a time, he became Edward's ideological touchstone. However, Hardie would become an ardent pacifist whereas Mick chose to fight.

Based on his upbringing and early privations he had a pronounced distaste for the upper classes[15] and this is of course not surprising. It was not long before he wanted to go abroad, away from England which he now considered torpid and unenlightened.[16] He then went to Turkey to work for the English Telephone company; Mick was playing croquet when war broke out. Along with others, he was interned in a Turkish prison until the Red Cross effected his release.

Mannock joined the Wellingborough Mock Parliament which served as the context in which he discovered he had a knack for oratory and leadership. He found he was able to provide food for thought for the men who had, prior to his arrival, been lethargic and indifferent to politics. Every night, he made a special point of stirring up criticism of the politicians and the way the war was being run[17] by the upper classes, whose poor decisions caused thousands to die in the trenches. He applied to the Royal Engineers, wanting nothing more to do with telephones, and was finally accepted by the Royal Engineers at the rank of Sergeant Major.[18] He was then transferred to Fenny Strafford for three months training.

He was at this point somewhat directionless. A pre-war friend, Eric Tomkins RFC, spotted him at the railway station. Over lemonades, Tomkins suggested Mick transfer to Netheravon on Salisbury Plain to train as a pilot.[19] According to Adrian Smith:

> 'Tompkins wasn't alone in portraying the skies above France as a jousting ground for the chivalrous knights of the air. By the summer of 1916 British newspapers were beginning to discover Albert Ball.'[20]

This raises an interesting subject; the notion of the ace in the public eye. As discussed, the French and Germans both promoted their aces in the media, deliberately crafting the iconic image of the ace to raise morale and promote national accomplishment. As we shall see in chapter 12, Jacques Mortane created a magazine that showcased the exploits of Allied aces, favouring his friend Georges Guynemer. However, the British, especially General Trenchard in command of the RAF, did not like the term 'ace' on grounds of morale, arguing that contributions of ordinary service personnel would be ignored in favour of the aces.[21]

Adrian Smith stated that Mannock transferred to aviation because he thought it more glamorous than the trenches.[22] However, Mick was not a man who valued glamour or 'shams of any kind'. Perhaps more to the point, aviation sounded or was imagined as being more *romantic* or chivalric than the trenches. Mick was a sensitive and shy man, who played the violin; glamour was the last thing on his mind.

EDWARD 'MICK' MANNOCK – COLLECTIVIST DOGFIGHTER

Mick initially thought he would not qualify for aviation due to his having only one good eye, but Tomkins peered at it and said it looked perfectly fine to him, which gave Mick the idea to apply anyway![23] He crept into the medical hut and memorized the eye chart; he passed and was fit for flying.[24]

Mannock transferred to the RFC shortly after his commission was confirmed in June 1916.[25] He gained his Aero club certificate 3895 on 28 November. In February 1917, he became a probationary flying officer.[26]

The relationship between Mick and James McCudden was cautious but friendly. Mick knew that McCudden was one of the few who could spin an Airco DH 2 and recover, provided it was not under 2,000ft. Mick took pleasure in proving McCudden only half right; you could recover from a spin in a DH 2 at low level.[27]

McCudden, writing years later, had this to say about Mannock; he claims his advice saved Mannock's life in contrast to Mick's assertion that he was only 'half-right':

> 'The pupils here during the period of which I write were very good. One I particularly remember named Mannock. One day he came to me and said that I was the cause of saving his life. I had only just previously given him instructions what to do if he unfortunately got into a "spin". He had just had his first spin and had remembered my advice, which I think at the time was to put all controls central and offer up a very short and quick prayer. Mannock was a typical example of the impetuous young Irishman, and I always thought he was of the type to do or die. He now holds the D.S.O. and M.C. and a bar, and at the time of writing has accounted for over two score of German machines.'[28]

Captain Meredith Thomas who Mick met at Joyce Green for his final phase of training, described him:

> 'My first impression of Micky was that he was very reserved, inclined to strong temper, but very patient and somewhat difficult to arouse...he was a very good conversationalist and liked discussions and arguing a point. He had strong likes and dislikes and was almost too serious-minded.'[29]

AERO-NEUROSIS

In March 1917, Mannock passed his pilot's test and was posted to Clarmarais, near St. Omer; it was here he began to keep a diary. His first plane there was the Bristol Scout which he liked immensely. He was billeted at the YMCA in St. Omer which he described as:

> 'Nasty town. Mainly composed of estaminets, old women and dirty – very dirty – children. The roads and streets remind one of Constantinople in their glistening filth. Went to the cinema in the evening. Horrible.'[30]

Mannock was posted to 40 squadron on 6 April which was stationed at Aire Lens and the Le Bassee sector. Life expectancy for a new pilot was 11 days.[31] The next day he soloed on Nieuport scouts, probably a Nieuport 17 C. 1 which he called a 'Lovely bus. Tootled around and went as far as the lines…' Mannock thought the Nieuport was a bit heavy on the controls compared to the Bristol.'[32]

Lionel Blaxland noted that:

> '…he [Mannock] was different. His manner, speech and familiarity were not liked. He seemed too cocky for his experience, which was nil. His arrival at the unit was not the best way to start. New men took their time and listened to the more experienced hands; Mannock was the complete opposite. He offered ideas about everything; how the war was going, how it should be fought, the role of the scout pilots, what was wrong or right with our machines. Most men in his position… would have shut up and earned their place in the mess.'[33]

On 19 April, Mick was practicing his shooting in his Nieuport 17 – his one good eye made this necessary if he was going to survive let alone excel in aerial combat. Mick found out the hard way about the sesquiplane's one big flaw; the single spar lower wing:

> 'Did some gun practice and in one dive from two thousand my right bottom plane broke and fell clean away. Managed to right the machine after desperate efforts with the "joy stick" and landed slowly and safely about half a mile away from aerodrome. Such a thing has never happened before where the pilot has not been killed or injured by the fall.'[34]

EDWARD 'MICK' MANNOCK – COLLECTIVIST DOGFIGHTER

Frederick Oughton, editor of Mannock's diary, notes that Mick was under pressure to get a kill. There was gossip that he shied away from fights as he was trying to get the hang of sighting his gun with only one eye. According to Sgt W. Bovett, rigger of planes for Mick's flight:

> 'his bottom plane came off in the air, while diving vertically at the ground target. By skilful piloting he managed to get the machine safely down, but crashed it in a ploughed field without being hurt. It was a splendid effort. I saw the whole thing happen.'

When the rigger reached the crash site, Mannock shocked and frightened him by accusing him of causing the accident (that it was the rigger's fault that the wing gave way), but seeing the rigger's face go grey, Mannock burst out laughing and cheered him up by showing him the defective strut socket which had broken.[35]

During his first two months in France flying Nieuports against seasoned Jastas, Mannock wrote the following; this is one of the first indications we have that Mick was beginning to suffer from his newly chosen vocation – 'wind up' refers to acute anxiety experienced by fliers:

> 'Over the lines today on Parry's bus. Engine cut out three times. Wind up. Now I can understand what a tremendous strain to the nervous system active service flying is. However cool a man may be there must always be more or less of a tension on the nerves under such trying conditions. When it is considered that seven out of ten forced landings are practically "write off's," and 50 per cent are cases where the pilot is injured, one can quite understand the strain of the whole business.'[36]

He also admitted to Jim Eyles that under fire for the first time he 'had the wind up' and confided to his mother that 'it's very lonely being up in the clouds all by one's self, with the anti-aircraft shells coughing and barking all around one...'[37]

Oughton notes that Mannock's anxiety caused at least two temporary breakdowns during his career at times when flying duties became arduous and dangerous. Prior to take off for patrol he often felt sick. After examining what was left of some of his early victims, he became afraid of dying as they had died. He had no wish to show his feelings in front of men ten years younger than himself, but whenever he heard of the death of a comrade, a deep and terrible Celtic sadness overtook him, and he would go and sit in his sleeping quarters, keening in the true Irish fashion, his head low over his knees as he wept, crying out the name of the dead man.[38] Oughton also notes that radical changes in the weather made Mannock feel unwell and feverish, due to his imprisonment in Turkey. At this time, he was still in a state of acute nervous tension, which reacted on his physical condition.[39] Malnutrition was an ongoing problem for front-line squadrons. The scarcity of fresh food meant that often mess officers had to hunt around for supplies, often bartering for it. One squadron used to transport eggs in boxes lashed to the undercarriage (bomb) rack of an aircraft![40]

Mick clearly had nervous exhaustion on the brain, so that he was keen to notice when other pilots became symptomatic. Whether this was true or not is a matter for further investigation. At the very least it was probably a source of comfort to Mannock that others were experiencing the same thing yet carried on just the same:

> 'Brown [this may be Roy Brown] and de Burgh left for England a few days ago. Brown showed signs of nerves – poor chap, I hope they both get soft jobs until the end of the war. MacKenzie will be next to break down, I think.'[41]

Taffy Jones, a contemporary and future friend of Mannock wrote:

> 'This spirit of "carry on" (from sports) found its counterparts in the RFC spirit. This aggressively offensive spirit could not tolerate sorrow, for sorrow was liable to lower the morale. Though it might hide in the bosom of the RFC pilot, it was only permitted to exude in the secret seclusion of his sleeping quarters. In the mess it was an unwritten law for pilots to forget their sorrow and assume a cheerfulness which gave the impression of "living for the day."'[42]

This is a key point that explains much of the perceived *carpe diem* spirit seen with First World War flying squadrons; the notion that pilots repressed their angst and inner turmoil and hid behind a mask of good cheer. This does not appear to be a singularly British cultural tendency, as it appears in writings of French, German, and American pilots. W.H.R. Rivers felt that those who fared best confronted their fears openly, like Udet, who survived

EDWARD 'MICK' MANNOCK – COLLECTIVIST DOGFIGHTER

the war with an intact psyche, and that those that didn't aggravated their psychological strain. Mannock both repressed and brooded and eventually confided his emotions to Jim Eyles which matches an observation made by Rivers:

> 'It often happens in cases of "war-neurosis," as in neurosis in general, that the sufferers do not suppress their painful thoughts, but brood over them constantly until their experience assumes vastly exaggerated and often distorted importance and significance. In such cases the greatest relief is afforded by the mere communication of these troubles to another…'[43]

The Battle of Arras took a heavy toll on the RFC. Although the British squadrons were still largely flying Nieuport 17s,[44] General Trenchard insisted on aggressive tactics. The RFC was tasked with artillery spotting, photography of trench systems and bombing. Aerial observation was hazardous work given the nature of the aircraft employed by the RFC at this time. Their misery was compounded by the arrival of Manfred von Richthofen's Jasta 11 in March 1917, which gave way to a period of high British losses known as 'Bloody April.' Ernst Junger later wrote:

> '…during these days, there was a whole series of dogfights, which almost invariably ended in defeat for the British since it was Richthofen's squadron they were up against. Often five or six planes in succession would be chased away or shot down in flames.'[45]

The average flying life of an RFC pilot in Arras during Bloody April was 18 hours. Between 4-8 April, the RFC lost 75 aircraft and 105 aircrew. On 9 May, Mannock was over the lines at Arras flying fifteen feet off the deck![46] Mannock achieved his first victory when he shot down a German observation balloon,[47] and was the only one to return properly to the aerodrome – his plane riddled with bullet holes. He noted in his diary, 'I don't want to go through such an experience again.'[48] After landing, Oughton noted that Mick got the news of Albert Ball's death at the hand of Lothar von Richthofen, the ambitious brother of the famous Red Baron.[49]

At dusk on 7 May, Captain Albert Ball (56 squadron RFC) and Lothar von Richthofen (Jasta 11) duelled with each other north of Douai. At the conclusion both were on the ground. Ball's S.E 5 (A4850) was seen to emerge from a low cloud inverted before hitting the ground; he died within minutes. Lothar made a forced landing in his Albatros D. III with holed fuel tanks. Ball was buried at Annoeullin cemetery, near the crash site. Lothar received credit for bringing Ball down although he claimed a 'Sopwith Triplane', not an S.E.5.[50]

Ball's body was free from wounds, giving rise to the belief by some that he was not shot down by the Red Baron's brother but was disoriented in the low cloud so that when he emerged, a crash was inevitable. Whether Lothar earned it or not, he received a fuel pipe and a Vickers machine gun (both of which contained a bullet hole) presumably from Ball's aeroplane that were later displayed at the Richthofen Museum in Schweidnitz.[51]

The battle for Arras continued at a fever pitch. Mick describes the slow erosion of his courage in the course of just one aerial battle. It would seem as though 'moral fibre'[52] or courage was an elusive and slippery phenomenon; strength of courage or 'pluck' was stronger on some days than others:

> 'We were sixteen thousand feet up at the time. I turned almost vertically on my tail – nose-dived and spun down towards our own lines, zig-zagging for all I was worth with machine guns crackling away behind me like mad. The engine picked up when I was about three thousand feet over Arras and the Huns for some reason or other had left me. I immediately ran into another Hun but hadn't the pluck to face him. I turned away and landed here with my knees shaking and my nerves all torn to bits. I feel a bit better now, but all my courage seems to have gone after that experience this morning.'[53]

Seeing the state Mannock was in, his C.O. took him off front line duty and had him ferry aircraft from St. Omer for the rest of the day. Even doing this simple task however he complained of more trouble with nerves. He also noted at this time that MacKenzie went on leave due to nerves and wondered if he would get that bad.[54] Mannock was careful to keep any hint of his suffering from the letters he sent to family and friends; he did not want the word to get out about his nervous state.[55] It is important to remember that many doctors and officers viewed a nervous condition as cowardice. The medical profession was still learning about combat trauma and the best the RFC could muster were two basic classifications: unable to fly, and unwilling to fly; physiological and psychological ailments being the former, cowardice the latter.

EDWARD 'MICK' MANNOCK – COLLECTIVIST DOGFIGHTER

In early June of 1917, Mannock's nerves were still bothering him, so that he wrote in his diary: 'Afraid I am breaking up...Captain Keen very decent. Let me off some flying for today. I think I'll take a book and wander into the woods this afternoon—although it rather threatens rain. O! for a fortnight in the country at home!'[56] It is interesting how his childhood love of books was still present even in the heat of combat. He also complained of problems sleeping, most likely, he thought, due to his 'sins'.[57] It is unclear as to the origin of these sins; did he feel guilty for killing people or for what would be termed during the Second World War as 'lack of moral fibre?' Bourke wrote that though 'many military and psychological commentators denied the importance of guilt, an equal number were forced to admit that such feelings sometimes precipitated war neuroses.'[58]

Mannock went on leave from 17 June to 20 July.[59] Shortly after his return from leave, he shot down a DFW two-seater south of Avion; it was his first close inspection of his handiwork as an air-fighter:

> '...my first few shots killed the pilot and wounded the observer... The machine was completely smashed, and rather interesting also was the little black and tan dog – dead – in the observer's seat. I felt exactly like a murderer.'[60]

According to Oughton, it was the sight of the dead dog that nauseated him far more than the human corpse, for he was still very fond of all animals, a legacy from his early youth.[61]

Mannock had to travel to the trenches near Avion to see the wreck of the DFW he shot down. He saw first-hand what trench warfare was like:

> The journey to the trenches was rather nauseating – dead men's legs stick through the sides with puttees and boots still on – bits of bones and skulls with the hair peeling off, and tons of equipment and clothing lying about. This sort of thing, together with the strong graveyard stench and the dead and mangled body combined to upset me for a few days.'[62]

On 12 August, Mannock fought Lt Joachim von Bertraub which he spelled incorrectly (Bartrap) in his diary:

> 'Had a splendid fight with a single seater Albatross Scout last week...this proved to be Lieutenant von Bartrap, Iron Cross...

AERO-NEUROSIS

> the scrap took place at two thousand feet up, well within view of the whole front. And the cheers! It took me five minutes to get him to go down, and I had to shoot him before he would land. I was very pleased that I did not kill him... his machine, a beautiful all black with crosses picked out in white lines.[63]

Bertraub favoured an Albatros D.III or Albatros D.V as his aircraft of choice. His personal mount was painted black or dark purple, with the Maltese Crosses edged in white and a comet painted on the side of the fuselage. Bertraub won both classes of the Iron Cross for his feats.[64]

> 'During the last few weeks, we have been issued with a new type of Nieuport machine. The tail plane and rudder are shaped very like a Hun scout, also the body is fish shaped (most likely Nieuport 27 B3607).'[65]

Mannock also mentions this new configuration was a source for much concern as these planes were often mistaken for German aircraft; the rounded tail of the Nieuport 27 may have made it appear like an Albatros or Pfalz fighter.

> 'Three American paper men came to visit us the other day, and the C.O. insisted on my telling the story of the flight. They were frightfully interested and took voluminous notes and begged for pieces of the wing as mementos. I am having a model of the Hun made out of the woodwork of one of the wings.'[66]

Oughton notes that as a the result of this interview Mannock's fame spread throughout America, and he was consequently better known in the US than in Britain.[67] Mannock shot down another German in his new Nieuport, saying the Nieuport was much quicker than the Hun. The German had gone down in flames...It was a horrible sight and made him feel sick.[68] After this, he ceased keeping a diary due to pressure of operations.

One considerable solace during this early period of nervous strain was music. He still carried a violin about with him, and spent hours listening to a recording of Kreisler playing Caprice Viennois, then trying to copy it, but the difficult passages always eluded him. 'Hell, I don't know how the bloody fellow does it,' he kept repeating. Regarding Mick's ability, William 'McScotch'MacLenachan, Mannock's good friend and 40 squadron-mate said:

EDWARD 'MICK' MANNOCK – COLLECTIVIST DOGFIGHTER

'Watching Mick's expressive face as he successfully accomplished the difficult double stopping passages in the Caprice, I was amazed at the emotional splendour of his playing. Technique was required, but there was something greater than that, something no other violinist had ever conveyed to me. Mick had the soul of an idealist, one that can endure agonies of mind and body for his ideals, can kill for his beliefs. He told us all this in his playing…many of the others were equally spellbound by the tall gaunt figure standing in the half-light at the far corner of the mess. On my telling him of this he refused to play for several days and when we finally persuaded him to do so he turned his face to the wall.'[69]

MacLenachan found a lost cat near the camp. Mick comforted it and gave it a dish of warm milk, and then picked it up, soothing away the shivers from the cold. While debating what to name it, the little feline urinated on Micks tunic, thus earning its name: Piddle![70]

It was at this time that the S.E 5a was introduced to squadron 40; the Nieuport was withdrawn much to Mick's disgust. He took a sharp-tongued dislike to the S.E 5a, because the engine was temperamental and often cut out. He said the so-called experts had grossly over-estimated the capabilities of the machine without first testing it in action.[71] This opinion was echoed by other British pilots such as Ball and Bishop regarding their affection for their trusty and nimble Nieuports.

Mannock protested to his Commanding Officer (CO) Major Leonard Tilney about the plane but failed to get any action or even a promise that something might be done to safeguard the lives of the pilots; he then changed tack and began filing negative reports about the S.E 5a; which had to be passed on as they were official documents. Before long, Mick's nemesis Major- General Sir Hugh Trenchard arrived, witnessing Mannock's return from a flight, after which Mannock complained in front of Tilney and Trenchard about the gun jamming again. 'Give me the Nieuport any day' was the upshot. Tilney urged Mick to show more respect and moderate his comments, but he replied: 'I'm sorry, sir, but if this results in me getting my good old Nieuport back, I don't care.'[72] The result of this meeting was that a gunnery officer from H.Q. was sent to look into the guns jamming, also Mick's outburst in front of Trenchard merely underscored his own feelings about the plane, so an investigation was launched.[73]

AERO-NEUROSIS

The following is a useful comparison of what planes the S.E were pitted against at the front:

> 'Albatros and Halberstadt – an S.E 5 could outfight these unless the Hun pilot was a particularly good one, so you could take these on any way you liked; Fokker D7 – as the Fokker could turn inside an S.E, you did not mill round in circles, but attacked from above and zoomed up from your height again. The S.E was very little faster than a Fokker, but it had an inferior climb; Fokker Triplane – it could turn inside and outclimb an S.E, so you treated it with more respect and adopted up-and-down tactics, although the S.E was faster.'[74]

During foul weather, Mannock's engine cut out and he made a forced landing on a frozen battlefield littered with dead bodies; he was sickened and upon returning to the base he looked pale and went to his quarters. MacLenachan followed him, knowing the tell-tale signs. He wiped his eyes, 'It's a miserable life, Mac. Do you know there's only one bright spot in the whole of my existence out here? …when you bought this bit of ribbon and had it sewn on my tunic.' 'It's high time you had a rest, Mick. Come on, let's go and have a drink.'[75]

Another instance of Mannock's compassion towards his friends took place on Christmas Day 1917, when his friend MacLenachan was intent on flying a mission but Mannock secretly disconnected his starting magneto to prevent him from potentially getting killed on Christmas Day.[76] Mannock also sensed that MacLenachan needed a rest by telling the Medical Officer that he was cracking up and needed a leave; resulting in them both going on leave together.[77]

As his leave was ending, Mannock went to the War Office in London and was told he was to remain in England as a flying instructor. He was furious and protested, but to no avail. While staying at the RFC Club in Bruton Street and bar-hopping he was introduced to General Sir David Henderson, who he persuaded to have him posted back to France, saying, 'If I can't get back to France soon with permission, I'll return without it, sir.' Henderson told him he'd be court-martialled; to which Mannock replied 'Death before dishonour!'[78] Unbeknownst to him, Major Alan Dore, acting CO of 74 Squadron, had already chosen Mannock to lead A Flight of 74 Squadron at London Colney, Hertfordshire, where he would serve as an instructor initially.[79]

EDWARD 'MICK' MANNOCK – COLLECTIVIST DOGFIGHTER

Mannock was instrumental in reducing the barriers between instructors and pupils. He knew that such aloofness was bad for new pilots. At the same time, he introduced a totally new approach to teaching using his combat experiences as guides. On the hangar walls he had the following slogan painted: 'Always above; Seldom on the same level; never underneath.'[80] The following is the first impression of what Ira 'Taffy' Jones, a future squadron mate and biographer of Mannock's, thought of him:

> 'His tall, lean figure; his weather-beaten face with its deep set Celtic blue eyes; his unruly dark brown hair; his modesty in dress and manner appealed to me, and immediately like all the other pupils, I came under his spell. He had a dominating personality, which radiated itself on all those around. Whatever he did or said compelled attention. It was obvious that he was a born leader of men.'[81]

Mannock stressed that practising stunting was a waste of time, focusing instead on the quick turn especially since they would be flying S.E 5as. While at London Colney, forging his pupils into a fighting unit he met 'Taffy' Jones, who stressed he fought for Christianity and freedom of thought and speech, and kindness to those who needed it.[82] These sentiments resonated with Mannock and he more or less adopted them as his own.

It was at this time that Mick began to obsess about the notion of his aeroplane catching fire. He asked Captain Cairns, commander of C Flight, what his first thought would be if his plane caught fire. Cairns didn't have an answer, but Mannock did. 'A bullet in the head.'[83] This was a first vocalization, meaning that given Mannock's psychological protocol of showing emotion only privately (in his room), he must have been tormenting himself about this quite a bit.

Less than a month later, the squadron moved to Tetengham, near Dunkirk for shooting practice, then Dixmude, where the squadron became anxious due to inactivity, until they were finally transferred to the Ypres Front in early April 1918. On 12 April, Mannock's flight shot down four Albatrosses out of eight. Although Mick got two of them, he gave credit to the whole flight.[84]

Mannock gleefully delivered the news of the Red Baron's death, scorning any notion of a toast to his supposed gallant foe; he in fact hoped the Red Baron had died as horrible a death as many of his comrades. 'Any hint of sentiment or honour was deemed pathetic, childish, and naïve: beyond memorial services and *Morning Post* obituaries, chivalry had no place in modern warfare'[85]

AERO-NEUROSIS

There were those who believed the Red Baron's tactics were cowardly, which could explain Mannock's hatred of the man as Mick was extremely intolerant of cowardice, knowing that this ran through every man's mind in varying degrees, saying to a green pilot who showed cowardice during a patrol, 'You left the flight just now when we were about to attack those Huns …' 'Yes sir, but I …' 'Well, you can't do that, I won't have it. It's cowardice and if you do it again, I'll shoot you down myself!'[86] Two days later, he fired shots over this same pilot's upper wing when he began to withdraw from a fight; after landing he tore the wings off the pilot's coat and had him transferred.[87]

Mannock was very self-effacing regarding this own flying. Others such as Taffy Jones related the following exciting description of him in action:

> 'In his first fight, which commenced at 12,000 feet, there were six Pfalz scouts flying east from Kemmel Hill direction. One he shot to pieces after firing a long burst…another he crashed; it spun into the ground after it had been hit by a deflection shot; the other, a silver bird, he had a fine set-to with, while his patrol watched the Master at work…first they waltzed around one another like a couple of turkey-cocks, Mick being tight on his adversary's tail. Then the Pfalz half rolled and fell a few hundred feet behind him. Mick followed, firing as soon as he got into position. The Hun then looped – Mick looped, too, coming out behind and above his opponent and firing short bursts. The Pfalz then spun - Mick spun also, firing as he spun. This shooting appeared to me to be a waste of ammunition. The Hun eventually followed out: Mick was fast on his tail – they were now down to 4,000 feet. The Pfalz now started twisting and turning, which was a sure sign of "wind up". After a sharp burst close up, Mick delivered the coup de grace, and poor old fellow went down headlong and crashed.'[88]

Mannock commented that he fired during the spin to increase 'wind up'. Commanding officer of 74 Squadron, Keith 'Grid' Caldwell assessed him as follows:

> 'His successes were largely due to his tactical approach to a fight and his extraordinarily fine deflection shooting once he was engaged. In an air fight most people try to get behind the other man to get an easier shot and where you cannot be shot

EDWARD 'MICK' MANNOCK – COLLECTIVIST DOGFIGHTER

at, but Mannock was able to hit them at an angle. With two-seaters he usually came down from an angle in front where the pilot's vision was obscured by the top wing, and if he missed in his approach, he half-rolled to come up under the tail and attack where the gunner had trouble getting at him.'[89]

Mannock was not a stunt pilot; Caldwell continues his observation of his no-nonsense style of flying:

'I never saw him looping or wasting energy or engine power in this manner, nor was he a better than average pilot. He really hated the Germans – there was absolutely no chivalry with him [at this time] and the only good Hun was a dead one. I am afraid we rather fostered this blood-thirsty attitude in 74 Squadron, because it helped to keep a war-going atmosphere which is essential for the less tough types.'[90]

In keeping with his 'good of the group' ethos, Mannock had an established habit of lining up kills for younger and less experienced pilots, which accounted for 25 enemy aircraft. At his death, Mannock had 73 kills but adding these other 25, it is close to one hundred. In contrast, von Richthofen shot down 80, and was known to claim planes which were merely damaged and force-landed as definite victories. He also claimed victories won by his pupils.[91]

Another example of Mannock's collectivist approach to air fighting was his ability and desire to save many a pilot by drawing the enemy away from attacks on squadron mates; this was true with Taffy Jones as well as Clements. When Taffy's gun jammed and he had an Albatros right on his tail, Mannock appeared from out of nowhere and finished off the Albatros in short order.[92] With Clements, he drew the enemy off his tail by doing an inverted spin, faking being out of control; after the Hun stopped the pursuit, he tore off for home.[93] Mannock's collectivist approach to air-fighting became increasingly the norm. The new orthodoxy shunned individual achievement, focusing on the need for teamwork.[94]

Flying at this pace day in, day out, was beginning to destroy Mannock's nerves. Things that before were only mildly annoying were now amplified to resemble genuine anxiety and deep depression. On increasingly more patrols he saw planes in flames, resulting in more repression with his 'sizzle

sizzle wonk' half-joke,[95] or more blatantly, 'I'll blow my brains out rather than go down roasting.'[96] Mannock's strategy for dealing with going down in flames by resorting to black humour was consistent with W. H. R. Rivers' hypothesis that repression or making light of deepest fears only made them worse.[97] Rivers argued that those that admitted that being fearless was impossible were more likely to survive, and that at least aviators had a psychological advantage in that they controlled their machines.[98]

By June 1918, his nerves were under the greatest strain. Taffy was on leave but when he returned he was shocked. Mannock's face was grey and haggard, he was brusque, and his body seemed to be 'coiled up'. Their first discussion after Taffy's return centred around whether Taffy was ready to die for his country 'in flames or in pieces'.[99] Here again, Mannock used sarcasm or black humour to express and ultimately exacerbate the inner turmoil he felt about being potentially burned alive.

Mannock needed another leave; it was rumoured that he would be posted perhaps to 85 squadron. He got his orders to replace Billy Bishop as head of 85 and he was also promoted to Major. The news didn't have much of an impact on him. On leave, Mannock visited the Eyles; they too were shocked upon seeing him. In particular, his eyes 'seemed to be burning with deep fires'. He wept frequently. He was obviously very ill, although he insisted he was still quite fit to serve. Jim Eyles recalled that Mannock:

> 'had changed dramatically. Gone was the old sparkle we knew so well; gone was the incessant wit. I could see him wring his hands together to conceal the shaking and twitching. [One day, as the time approached for Mannock to return to the war] he started to tremble violently. This grew into a convulsive straining. His face, when he lifted it, was a terrible sight. Saliva and tears were running down his face; he couldn't stop it. His collar and shirt-front were soaked through. He smiled weakly at me when he saw me watching and tried to make light of it; he would not talk about it at all. I felt helpless not being able to do anything. He was ashamed to let me see him in this condition but could not help it, however hard he tried.'[100]

The Eyles fed and cared for him, but Mannock remained 'submerged in his own sadness'.[101] On 3 July he departed for France for the last time; like Udet and Springs,'the fight' was all he lived for now. When he left, Eyles sensed he would not see his friend again.[102]

EDWARD 'MICK' MANNOCK – COLLECTIVIST DOGFIGHTER

Major Mannock returned as commander of 85 Squadron. His one dictum, repeated many times during briefings and in the mess, ran, 'To fight is not enough, you must kill!' Those who took no notice of him were ruthlessly posted away to bombing and reconnaissance duties.[103] All things considered, Mannock managed to maintain an aggressive attitude outwardly to his squadron. Things seemed to be going well enough when he was told that McCudden was dead, killed during take-off to assume command of 60 Squadron.[104] In terms of scores and fame, McCudden, Ball and Bishop had all been contemporaries of Mannock; seeing them die one after the next exacerbated his suffering. There was no more telling oneself that at least this man, who had similar experiences and victories, was still alive. McCudden had written about his own combat flying:

> 'I always take a great personal interest in my machine, and I was rewarded by the knowledge that my machine was as fast and would climb as well as any other in the squadron…I am a stickler for detail in every respect, for in aerial fighting I am sure it is the detail that counts more than the actual fighting points.'[105]

In spite of McCudden's careful preparations it still wasn't enough, as human beings cannot maintain at all times the type of concentration required to stay alive in combat indefinitely; sooner or later a pilot has a bad day and it can be fatal. Mannock sublimated his anguish over losing McCudden into an increasingly aggressive attitude towards shooting down Germans. At 85 Squadron, he duelled with Taffy Jones (now commanding A Flight 74 Squadron) over victories. The object here was to shoot down as many Germans as possible as a tribute to McCudden.[106] One day over lunch Mannock told Taffy that he had caught up to Bishop's score; 72. 'They'll have the red carpet out for you when you get back to England after the war.' Mannock replied, 'There won't be any "after the war" for me.'[107] He sensed that either the desire for those things worth living for was completely gone, or that his transformation was complete, that he was inescapably a creature of the war context. Like Paul Baumer in *All Quiet*, nowhere else made any sense to him anymore. Mick mentioned that at one point he had thought about getting married, but finally gave in to the notion that this was not in the cards for him[108] – he had nothing left to offer another.

According to William MacLanachan:

> 'Behind Mannock's frank contempt of the Germans lay a deeper subconscious instinct of distrust and hatred of the

aggressive bullying militaristic spirit of Prussianism...he was fighting for a cause, for a better world order, and he saw the German militarism as the greatest obstacle to that ideal.'[109]

Mannock wrote a letter to Mary Lewis shortly before his final patrol. Contained in this excerpt is the notion that physical and mental anguish served a purpose; that Mannock sublimated his anxieties as a test of character:

> 'I do not believe that the war & the "Great Push" are things "rare and superficial." Don't you see my dear child that strife & bloodshed & physical "exertion" & mental anguish are all good, gloriously wonderfully beneficial things for the human race, just exactly the same as you and I experience when we are called upon by our sense of righteousness to resist some animal temptation? These boys out here fighting are tempted at every moment of their day to run away from the ghastly Hell created by the Maker, but they resist the temptation and die for it, or become fitter & better for it, or because of it.'[110]

At lunch, Sister Flanagan, one of two nurses who was regularly invited to take tea with 85 Squadron said, 'You're very casual about this dangerous game of yours, Mick. Aren't you ever afraid?' He looked fondly at her and his hard expression softened. 'We've got a job to do, my dear, and the cooler you are the more successful you'll be. And as to being frightened – I'm just like any other pilot. I'm scared stiff when I see my Hun floating down in flames.' He grimaced and was tense again. 'God will thank us in his own way for fighting – and if necessary dying – for Christianity and freedom. But I'm getting morbid...' He then turned to Lt Donald Inglis from New Zealand. 'Have you got a Hun yet, Kiwi?' 'No sir' 'Come on—.'[111]

Mannock took off but Inglis wasn't able to due to a jammed elevator; the flight was postponed until the next day. Mannock went to dinner where he met Taffy who asked him how he was feeling. He replied, 'I don't feel I shall last much longer, Taffy, old lad. If I'm killed I shall be in good company. You watch yourself. Don't go following any Huns too low or you'll join the sizzle-brigade with me.'[112]

Just before dawn while waiting for Inglis, Oughton wrote that Mannock played a well-worn recording of the Londonderry Air (Danny Boy) while smoking his pipe. At ten minutes to five they took off in no clouds.

EDWARD 'MICK' MANNOCK – COLLECTIVIST DOGFIGHTER

His instructions to Inglis were simple; keep close on my tail and do what I do. The two planes flew off into the early light over Pacut Wood when suddenly Mannock's plane made a steep starboard bank and reversed direction – Inglis watched, puzzled, but followed suit. Mannock dived steeply, guns firing and then zoomed away in a steep turn. Inglis was amazed to see an LVG coming into his sights. He waited until he was very close and then fired into the LVG's fuel tank; the plane burst into flames. Mannock broke his own rule and followed the plane down until they began taking fire from the ground. Inglis noticed that Mannock's plane had ceased jinking (taking evasive action) and began a lazy right hand bank. An orange flame spurted out of the starboard side of his's S.E 5a. The left wing now swung over and the plane went into the ground, exploding in flames near Merville. Inglis could not believe what he had seen but had trouble himself when his own fuel and oil tank were punctured, causing him to land close to British lines.[113] Inglis noted that 'all I could say when I got into the trench was that the bloody bastards had shot my Major down in flames.'[114]

During the last months of Mannock's life, it seemed as if he were taking risks that would accelerate his chances of being shot down. Seemingly he just wanted it to end, one way or another. J.T. MacCurdy in *War Neurosis* and Cambridge psychologist F. C. Bartlett argued that a combination of prolonged fatigue and acute stress provoked periodic disorientation and a morbid fatalism, whereby death came as a release.[115] Bartlett suggested that 'there generally has to be some final accident to bring about collapse' but based on what happened to Brown, Springs, and Lambert this was not the case; it was more of a slow burn with the tipping moment occurring most probably in the subconscious mind. Smith asserts that Mannock never did experience 'the collapse'[116] such as Lambert's but he did suffer grievously, experiencing episodic breakdowns then rallying. Apparently, the breakdowns had a cumulative effect; increasing in intensity as time wore on. RAF psychiatrist squadron leader E.W. Craig lists 18 'causes which, in his judgement, led to nervous breakdown in flying personnel'. Nine were directly applicable to Mannock's condition, including four of the top five[117] The following are the paraphrased eighteen reasons Craig reported as causing break down of combat pilots:

1) Flying at high altitudes.
2) Flying at low altitudes.
3) Long periods of flying without leave.
4) Returning to flying duty within a short period after illness.

5) Returning to flying duty within a short period after a crash.
6) Excessive use of alcohol.
7) Excessive use of tobacco.
8) Insufficient training.
9) Conditions which impair or impede free passage of air to the lungs.
10) Night flying.
11) Severe mental stress, fear, worry, anxiety.
12) Unsuitable employment; e.g. fighter pilots being assigned to bomber duty and vice versa.
13) Youth and immaturity.
14) Causes which lower morale; e.g. many casualties, lack of confidence in certain aeroplanes.
15) Responsibility—a commander's burden for entire flight, a death, etc.
16) Neurasthenia. Brooding over trivial matters in connection with ones work. Ability to do certain things, obsessions.
17) Severe physical strain.
18) Insomnia. Early morning patrols during summer months, lack of sleep.[118]

Mannock was awarded the Victoria Cross on 18 July 1919 due to the efforts of the Secretary for Air, Winston Churchill.[119] Mannock's tally in the Victoria Cross gallery at the Royal Air Force Museum is 73 victories.[120]

In conclusion, Mick Mannock was a sensitive, compassionate man who championed a collectivist approach to fighter tactics, focusing on the good of the group versus individual achievement. The strain of combat privately reduced this man to a shaking, nervous wreck. Outwardly he remained cheerful while leading his squadron and shooting down Germans and in allowing this dichotomy to exist, he accelerated his deterioration. His biggest fear and obsession was going down in flames which due to his exhausted state and the odds became self-fulfilling prophecy.

Chapter 12

The Unlikely Ace of Aces – Georges Guynemer

If men such as Boelcke, Ball and von Richthofen were the archetypal ace, physically fit, sportsmen, healthy and robust, Georges Guynemer grew up weak, pale, and slightly effeminate, the opposite of the stereotype. Perhaps that is part of the reason for his enduring appeal and near god-like status in France; it was easy for the average Frenchman to imagine achieving a similar trajectory. Nobody ever thought he would amount to anything, and he ended up being one of France's top aces, a testament and triumph of spirit and will power over physical strength. In the end however; his nerves ultimately got the better of him but not before he achieved 53 victories. Although statistically he did not achieve as many victories as Renè Fonck, France's highest scoring ace, he (unlike the arrogant and socially awkward Fonck) was beloved by all of France, right down to the smallest child. In a letter from a French schoolboy, the sentiments of the entire nation are expressed:

> 'Guynemer is the Roland of our epoch: like Roland he was very brave, and like Roland he died for France. But his exploits are not a legend like those of Roland, and in telling them just as they happened we find them more beautiful than any we could imagine. To do honor to him they are going to write his name in the Pantheon among the other great names. His aeroplane has been placed in the Invalides. In our school we consecrated a day to him. This morning as soon as we reached the school we put his photograph up on the wall; for our moral lesson we learned by heart his last mention in the despatches; for our writing lesson we wrote his name, and he was the subject for our them; and finally, we had to draw an aeroplane. We did not begin to think of him only after he was dead; before he died, in

our school, every time he brought down an aeroplane we were proud and happy. But when we heard that he was dead, we were as sad as if one of our own family had died.

'Roland was the example for all the knights in history. Guynemer should be the example for Frenchman now, and each one will try to imitate him and will remember him as we have remembered Roland. I, especially, I shall never forget him, for I shall remember that he died for France, like my dear Papa'.[1]

This passage contains many interesting aspects regarding the need for modern chivalry in France; the connection between Roland and Guynemer underscores the notion that French tradition of chivalric splendour had continuity, now and then. Also, for characteristics peculiar to the individual (Guynemer) all of France resonated with this young slight man, whose round black eyes seem to shine with a sombre brilliance.[2] A mortal man, but burnished and elevated by tracts by Boudreaux, Mortane, and the leadership and people of France in the hopes of lifting France's spirit from the awful news reports from the Western Front. In addition, Guynemer's successes helped assuage the residual animosity felt by the French people towards Germany regarding their defeat at the conclusion of the Franco-Prussian war, coupled with a nagging perception of faded glory characterized by the end of the Belle Epoque era. Also implicit in this schoolboy's essay is the notion that France will be ultimately victorious. Even though Roland perished and became an instant martyr, Charlemagne was ultimately victorious; just as France's trusted warrior Guynemer, had perished, so too would France achieve final victory over the Germans. Needless to say, Guynemer, like Roland, became a martyr for France. Much of the imagery concerning the fallen warrior undergirds this ethos – for example Lucien H. Jonas' work *Les heros de l'air ne Meurent pas* and the tracts written by Bordeaux and Mortane certainly helped create the mythology of the warrior martyr. There is no doubt that the mythologizing of Guynemer served the national purpose of winning the war and keeping morale high as well as undergirding the notion that it was all part of French manifest destiny. However, examining Guynemer as a human being – the good with the bad – is far more interesting and fair.

Georges Guynemer was born in Paris on Christmas Eve 1894. He saw then, and always, the faces of three women, his mother and his two elder sisters, standing guard over his happiness.[3] His father, Paul Guynemer, was

THE UNLIKELY ACE OF ACES – GEORGES GUYNEMER

a former officer and historian of the Cartulaire de Royallieu (historical society of Compiègne) and contributor to their publication *Le Seigneurie d'Offemont*.[4] When only a few months old, Georges had almost died of infantile enteritis.[5] His parents quickly took him to Switzerland, and then to Hyères to keep him in warm and humid conditions. The family lived in Compiègne, and Georges was raised mostly by his doting mother and two sisters. Too pretty and too frail, with his curls and his dainty little frock, he had an *'air de princesse'*.[6] He was educated at home by private tutor until he was nine, after which he attended school in Compiègne.[7]

Young Georges would walk through Compiègne with his father, who would share the town's rich history; the treaties that were signed, kings who were crowned, the magnificent fetes of Louis XIV, Louis XV, Napoleon I, and Napoleon III. On the Place de l'Hotel de Ville, Georges was taken with the bronze statue of Jeanne d'Arc. Paul Guynemer attended Stanislas College, in Paris and he wanted Georges to follow in his footsteps. The college registers note that young Georges had:

> 'a clear, active, well-balanced mind, but that he was thoughtless, mischief-making, disorderly, careless; that he did not work, and was undisciplined, though without any malice; that he was very proud, and ambitious to attain first rank.'[8]

Guynemer, although frail, also displayed 'agility, cleverness, a quick eye, caution, and a talent for strategy. He played his game... not liking to receive any suggestions... intending to follow his own ideas.'[9] Even at an early age, Guynemer was nervous which made him stutter sometimes when talking though his speech was 'vibrant, trenchant, like hammerstrokes, and he said things to which there was no answer. He had a horror of discussion: he was already all action'.[10] Like so many would be fliers, Guynemer was entranced by aviation:

> 'When an aeroplane flew over the quarter, Guynemer followed it with his eyes, and continued to gaze at the sky for some time after its disappearance. His desk contained a whole collection of volumes and photographs concerning aviation. He had resolved to go up some day in an aeroplane, and when his father asked what he wanted to do after his graduation his answer was simple: aviator. To which his father chided that this was a sport not a profession.[11] Guynemer persisted, explaining

to his father that: "That is my sole passion. One morning in the courtyard at Stanislas I saw an aeroplane flying. I don't know what happened to me: I felt an emotion so profound that it was almost religious."'[12]

War erupted while the Guynemer family was vacationing in Biarritz. Georges tried to enlist at once but was rejected twice due to his frailty; he needed to be 'built up' some more before being accepted.[13] Georges was quietly furious, and sulked as he watched relatives and friends answer the call. He finally made his way to Pau to enlist in the aviation corps (as aviation was no longer a sport but a profession due to the war), pleading with Captain Bernard-Thierry to let him serve, doing anything. The Captain replied finally, 'I can take you as student *mechanician*.'[14] The frail, pale child of Compiègne and Biarritz had a rough apprenticeship, sleeping on the floor, doing the dirtiest work about camp, cleaning engine cylinders and carrying cans of petrol.[15] He began to grow stronger, and learned every piece of an aeroplane, spending countless hours disassembling and reassembling until he understood how everything worked. Guynemer's biographer Henry Bordeaux wrote:

> 'As a painter grinds his colours before making use of them, so Guynemer's prelude to his future flights was to touch with his hands – those long white hands of the rich student, now tanned and calloused, often coated with soot or grease, and worthy to be the hands of a labourer – every piece, every bolt and screw of these machines which were to release him from his voluntary servitude.'[16]

A future comrade, Sous-Lieutenant Marcel Vaillet, noted, 'His highly interested little face amused us. When we landed, he watched us with such admiration and envy! He asked us endless questions and constantly wanted explanations. Without seeming to do so, he was learning.'[17] Through his father's connections in the military, Guynemer was promoted to student pilot on 26 January 1915. He began on Bleriot 'Penguins'[18] which were followed by short hops in full sized Bleriot XIs. His flight instructor Paul Tarascon said, 'He was very nervous, very excited. But he liked it; he swore only by aviation, he was a flying addict!'[19] Guynemer's first flight was on 10 March 1915,[20] the next day he received his diploma from the Aero club.

THE UNLIKELY ACE OF ACES – GEORGES GUYNEMER

On 8 June, Corporal Georges Guynemer was designated as a member of Escadrille MS.3, which he joined next day at Vauciennes.[21] According to Charles Vedrines, adjutant to squadron leader Antonin Brocard, Guynemer had some initial difficulty:

> 'The first flight made by Guynemer did not match our expectations, certainly not. The machine crashed on landing. Some found this incident very funny, because this child, who came among men and almost never opened his mouth, did not have an excellent reputation…I did not know what to think. Guynemer took up another plane with the same result. This perseverance was becoming alarming. We could…not allow this neophyte to demolish all the squadron's planes…This boy weighed only 48 kilograms, was a real bundle of nerves and, fearing ridicule from the others decided to confess his fears to the man who was perhaps the most brutal, but the best disposed towards him. So he came to me and said "you do not know me, but if you did, you'd know how I would love to do the things right!"[22] Brocard conceded, but said if he didn't learn to fly in two weeks—he would be washed out!'

Bordeaux, in his efforts to mythologize Guynemer, claimed these accidents did not occur but however provides no documentation to support his assertions. Under Vedrines' tutelage, Guynemer improved and executed his first observation mission over the Front in a Morane Type L Parasol on 13 June 1915.[23] MS. 3 began receiving two-seater Nieuport Xs and on 3 July, Brocard shot down a German plane over Compiègne with his rifle, which was the squadron's first victory and Guynemer had played a major role.[24]

After returning shot up from numerous reconnaissance patrols over the Front, Major Brocard felt Guynemer was 'very young: his extraordinary self-confidence and natural qualities will very soon make him an excellent pilot. …'[25] Guynemer's first victory over an Aviatik B from Flieger Abteilung 26 was on 19 July:

> 'We dived and took station 50 metres below, behind and to his left. After the first shots, the Aviatik swerved and we saw small pieces of debris falling away. The enemy observer responded

with a rifle, one bullet hit our wing, a second grazed Guerder's hand and a third grazed his head. In our final salvo, the pilot collapsed in the fuselage, the observer raised his arms and the Aviatik dived abruptly, in flames, between the trenches.'[26]

Guynemer was flying Morane Parasol No. 376 and landed in French territory close to where his victim fell. The Medaille Militaire was awarded to Guynemer and his observer (Charles Guerder) on 4 August, which was accompanied by the following statement:

'Corporal Guynemer: a pilot full of spirit and audacity, volunteering for the most dangerous missions. After a hot pursuit, gave battle to a German aeroplane, which ended in the burning and destruction of the latter.'[27]

When he finally obtained the longed-for Nieuport X, he flew sixteen hours in five days, and naturally went to parade himself over Compiègne. Without this dedication to his home, Guynemer felt the machine would never be consecrated.[28] Until the middle of September, he piloted two-seated Nieuport Xs, carrying one passenger, either as observer or combatant. At last he went up in his one-seated Nieuport and he enjoyed being at last alone with his machine and the sky.[29]

On 10 October, Guynemer was assigned Nieuport X no. 320, the former plane of Sergeant Armand Bonnard, who had named his plane *Vieux Charles*, perhaps in homage to the oldest pilot of the squadron Charles Jules Vedrines;[30] Guynemer kept the name, such was his affection for Vedrines. This aircraft was a single seat conversion of the factory issue Nieuport X.

After his fourth victory, Guynemer had to collect a new plane from Le Bourget airfield. A sports journalist, Jacques Mortane, met him at this time and began a trusted relationship between the two men at a café.[31] Guynemer received a great present on his twenty-first birthday – the Legion d'Honneur. After more victories, he was promoted to Sous-Lieutenant on 4 March 1916.[32] The following day, he wrecked the first *Vieux Charles*, replacing it with Nieuport XI No. 836. On 12 March, N.3 sent some of its best pilots to Boncourt-sur-Meuse to aid the Verdun defence and the following day, he suffered wounds to the arm and face from defensive fire from German two-seaters he had attacked. He was hospitalized in the Hotel Astoria in Paris.[33] His sister said that he exposed himself to German fire because:

THE UNLIKELY ACE OF ACES – GEORGES GUYNEMER

> 'This is how I master my nerves, little sister, mine are well tamed and I am now master. The Boche shot five hundred rounds at me as I manoeuvred... It was necessary, I accept that. My life was decided that morning. Without facing up to it I would have chickened out.'[34]

He was flying again by 18 May, in the third *Vieux Charles* (Nieuport X No. 328).

In April, N.3 was moved to Cachy to support the British Somme offensive which was designed to alleviate pressure on Verdun. The German fighters, still Fokker Eindeckers, were by then obsolete compared with the Nieuport 17, delivered to the French squadrons during early summer 1916.[35] Moreover, Immelmann had been killed in one performing his signature manoeuvre in June, extinguishing any remaining confidence in the E.III. Guynemer received two Nieuport 17s during the summer (*Vieux Charles* 4 &5); he scored five victories in these planes by September. Other aces in the 'Storks' were Jean Navarre, Mathieu de la Tour, Alfred Heurtaux, Rene Dorme, Albert Deuillin, and others. It was the premiere French squadron and naturally the first pre-production Spad VIIs were delivered to Escadrille N3 during late August 1916.[36]

The Spad VII marked a departure in aircraft construction and tactics. It was not a 'turn fighter' like the Nieuports, it was instead fast and rugged and featured an inline Hispano Suiza engine (Nieuports had 80 and 110 hp Le Rhone rotaries). Guynemer saw the potential of the new plane and participated in its development and he began a long correspondence with its designer, Louis Bechereau.[37]

Guynemer used a simple tactic; he approached the enemy at high speed and at close range he would fire a short burst – all of this occurred in the blink of an eye. He was self-deprecating regarding his piloting skills,[38] instead of focusing on flying only to acquire an advantageous firing position; he used the Spad to its fullest advantage and did not make the fatal mistake of trying to fly it like a Nieuport.

On the ground, several witnesses described him as an extremely dynamic man: 'A bundle of nerves, a guy full of energy'. He was not very popular with his mechanics, who he easily snubbed and his relationships with other pilots was sometimes 'quite lively' due to his refusal to share victories (unlike Mannock).[39] Rene Fisch, a fighter pilot of N.23 who had one victory, stated:

> 'Guynemer was not loved by us, because he was very remote and self-centred. As soon as he [and a couple of wingmen] went into battle if the plane was shot down, it was a plane for Guynemer.'[40]

AERO-NEUROSIS

Maurice Delporte, a modest ferry pilot, said for his part that Guynemer was not friendly '…he was not chic, even with pilots of his own escadrille.' The question of the confirmation of his victories was so sensitive to him that he even installed an experimental Kodak camera on his plane to document his victories.[41]

Jacques Mortane, who had thus far only written for various national newspapers, launched on 16 November 1916 his own weekly magazine *La Guerre Aerienne Illustree* (The Air War Illustrated) which would discuss the flying aces and their exploits. Guynemer was the first aviator centrefold poster! He was the subject of many subsequent articles which helped to cultivate and elevate his fame; for the ordinary French soldier (*poilu*) he acquired the status of a demigod.[42]

Heurtaux remembered the pleasant side of Guynemer's fame:

> 'The number of invitations we received…it was like being a famous singer. We put the letters in a heap on the squadron table. Each of us know which their personal letters of interest were. Then, we opened the other letters together…on nights when I went out with Guynemer, we would find jewellery in the pockets of our overcoats, with addresses …sometimes we had letters from children. So we sent them the gifts we'd received, an exchange of favours.'[43]

Fame had its price then as it does now; privacy became a precious commodity. In the biography written by Jules Roy in 1986, Roy quotes, from 'reliable evidence', that Guynemer had an affair with a certain Madame de Cornois during his early military career at Vauciennes. This married woman, whose husband had been mobilized, became pregnant, thus ending the affair.[44]

The most famous aspect of Guynemer's personal life was his relationship with the actress Yvonne Wignolle, aka Yvonne Printemps, well known to Paris at the time, as reported by the famous French actress Arletty: 'Everyone knew, we all said she was lucky; a flying ace, the youngest, the most famous, she would have been wrong to refuse…'[45]

On 11 July, N.3 moved to Bergues aerodrome in Flanders to support the Passchendaele offensive; for Guynemer it began badly as he had contracted bronchitis on the Aisne, resulting in his hospitalization in Dunkerque. Charles Nungesser, the second highest scoring French ace, was based in the sector but he and Guynemer were jealous of each other and avoided meeting.[46] Incidentally, he was very near where Roy Brown was stationed at Saint Pol-sur-Mer.

THE UNLIKELY ACE OF ACES – GEORGES GUYNEMER

On 13 July 1917, Guynemer witnessed the demonstration of a Sopwith triplane but the attempt of the pilot, Lt De Vaisseau Henri Barbier, to give a spectacular take off resulted in a stall and spin, breaking up as it hit the ground. Guynemer was deeply affected by this tragedy and kept repeating 'I, who had never seen a plane crash...'[47] Perhaps the very real danger of his profession began to sink in.

On 20 August 1917, he scored his 53rd and final victory, a DFW, while flying a new Spad XIII. His plane was damaged by friendly fire, and he then went on leave to Paris in late August. Several testimonies agree that he was very tired. Jacques Viguier, a fighter pilot, described seeing him in Paris: 'I followed him for quite a while. He looked like death, slightly stooped, worn out by combat.'[48] Jeanne Tournier, a journalist, noted that 'We too, found him pale. And the eyes, especially, confused us; very black, very shiny, and staring straight ahead...'[49]

Guynemer was tired of his fame and his former commandant of the Pau flying school, Bernard-Thierry noted:

> 'I invited my ex-student to dinner at the Madeleine...upon his entry the public gave him an ovation...the orchestra stopped what they were playing and replaced it with the Marseillaise... it was almost impossible to dine, with an endless stream of guests asking for autographs, on their menus or postcards. The ladies leant over Guynemer, wanting to touch or graze against him, Some kissed his uniform, his long row of medal ribbons, with countless palms, and when we had finished dinner, the entire room stood up again.'[50]

Guynemer was a dedicated Catholic; and prayed at every church he happened upon. He confided in the vicar of St. Pierre de Chaillot, a church that Guynemer regularly attended that 'This is fatal, I will not get out...' He did say to his comrade Battesti on 31 August that 'If I survive, I'm getting married and I will be a good father...'[51] Mortane stated that Guynemer flew between five and six hours a day:

> 'trying to overcome his bad luck. It was a hard time for him, but he would not give up. Like the skilled gambler who tries to win by continuing his betting, he fought over and over again, but could not add a single one to his many victories.'[52]

AERO-NEUROSIS

He visited his family in Compiègne, who found him very weakened. His father urged him to take a position as an instructor, he had done enough; to which Guynemer made the now famous comment: 'If you have not given everything, you have given nothing.'[53] This makes a great epigram, but judging from his last comment about getting married, I think he was conflicted and felt as though fate must now decide what happened to him and it did. His final flight was 11 September 1917 and he was most likely tired or upset due to the frustrations he had experienced in the last few days, such that he took risks he wouldn't have ordinarily taken or failed to manoeuvre his plane in the two seater's blind spot, such that a bullet fired by the gunner hit him in the head, killing him instantly or soon after the fatal bullet struck.[54] Perhaps he, like so many others, just wanted it to be over.

Jacques Mortane made the following very succinct observation about Guynemer: 'Guynemer was merely a powerful idea in a very frail body, and I lived near him with the secret sorrow of knowing that someday the idea would slay its container.'[55] The following is an excerpt from an interview with Guynemer by Mortane, shortly before the ace's death:

> 'The public as a rule has a misconception about air fighting and combat pilots. They very easily imagine that we are way up there relaxed, directing dogfights, and that the nearer we are to heaven the more invested we are with Divine Power. It is the journalists job to educate their readers and prevent them from harboring opinions as wrong as they are pitiable. I cannot verbally express the enervation I feel when hearing these misconceptions directed at me, in the form of compliments, to which I am compelled to grin and bear it. I would like to shout: "But, my poor fellow, you ought not to speak about this subject, for you know nothing whatever about it. You do not understand the first word of it, and you can hardly believe how little your eulogies flatter me, under the circumstances." But if I responded like this, no one would think of honouring my sincerity, or my desire to spread correct information – instead, everyone would think I was rude, pretentious, boastful, or something worse. This is the reason that I listen, remain quiet and let the enervation gnaw at me. Some tell me: It is better not to explain how fliers conduct their business in a dogfight. If the layman knew what we know, he would possibly no longer admire us.'[56]

THE UNLIKELY ACE OF ACES – GEORGES GUYNEMER

The last sentence alludes to what air fighting had become by this time; 'scientific murder' to quote Eddie Rickenbacker. Guynemer knew it, that the business of air-fighting was become more and more codified and less romantic. Guynemer liked precision flying so increased structure in tactics worked well for him. The Spad XIII was a stable and potent gun platform; pilots attacked from superior height at great speed, aimed carefully and fired at the last moment flashing by at high speed then zooming up to repeat the attack, or allow the next pilot in the flight to make an attack. The tactics created by the close of the First World War would provide a solid foundation for every subsequent air war.

Conclusions

In conclusion, by the late nineteenth and early twentieth centuries, men accustomed to the relatively calm life in their respective hometowns suffered a shock when confronted by the 'tech shock' of fully realized, mechanized warfare at the Western Front. Their psyches and nervous systems were ill prepared for what awaited them. Scientists and inventors riding the wave of the industrial revolution and in the spirit of the inventiveness of the times produced all manner of products, but seemingly no one understood the big picture, that if war broke out; many of these inventions would be used. Weapons such as U-boats, Zeppelins, tanks, aeroplanes, and most notably vast amounts of artillery were all used for the first time during the Great War. The wounds inflicted by these weapons, especially large calibre artillery, was a new phenomenon. It was seemingly an invisible war fought by machines, be they tanks, U-boats, aeroplanes; the enemy rarely had a face, making it easier to continue the slaughter, and in contrast, when the enemy had a face, psychological trauma often resulted. The human body was devastated – literally blown to bits – and this too had a profound effect on the collective psychology of those who witnessed it.

Air fighters seemed romantic and at times chivalrous compared with the misery experienced by those in the trenches, giving birth to a new breed of hero that both the public and those in the trenches craved; the ace. These aces were competitive and as the war progressed were both intoxicated and horrified by what was occurring in the skies above France. The mythology of their image helped the troops and the public foster hope in a war that defied explanation as to outcome, purpose, and duration. Those who fought in the air above France knew that what they were doing was best done during the summer of their lives. Arthur Gould Lee had this to say about his experience as an RAF pilot during the Great War:

CONCLUSIONS

> 'And to those of us who were to pass safely through this strife and bloodshed would be affected by it all the rest of our lives...and although maybe I'd not matched up in achievement with the best, I was there with them. It was my crowded hour of glorious life.'[1]

There was an intimacy in this new type of warfare that was different from trench warfare; aircraft of the various aces were recognizable, and even lesser pilots were identifiable if you knew what to look for. However, watching comrades and foes fall in flames in a disintegrating aeroplane affected those who witnessed it; pilots like Mannock would obsess and eventually die in the manner he feared most. Uniformly, pilots who actually viewed their victims were shaken; Roy Brown checked into hospital nine days after seeing the body of the Red Baron, his nerves and conscience had reached its limit. Moreover, when these pilots confronted their humanity they suffered greatly. Those who addressed it quickly fared better; those who repressed these feelings and events suffered exponentially. Those that were able to sublimate the horrors of war endured longer than those who could not.

Aviation psychiatry evolved with the war and was frustrated by inadequate diagnosis, treatment, and infrastructure but these improved by the war's conclusion. The lessons of the war were by no means codified, although countries like the US and Britain tried to express what they had learned in an effort to advance both aviation psychiatry and aviation in general. Many of those that flew and fought during the First World War would most likely not have been admitted as military pilots today. Modern training is rigorous, and understanding of PTSD by flight surgeons, psychologists, and psychiatrists make selection for this type of duty very selective. Even still, the horrors of war cannot be trained away – or forgotten – now or then.

Remarque commented in *All Quiet* about the aftermath of the war for those in the trenches:

> 'How to be returned home in 1916, out of the suffering and the strength of our experience we might have unleashed a storm. Now if we go back we will be weary, broken, burnt out, rootless, and without hope. We will not be able to find our way anymore. And men will not understand us – for the generation that grew up before us, though it has passed these years with us already had a home and a calling; now will return to its old occupations, and there will be forgotten--and the generation that has grown up after us will be strange to us and push us aside.'[2]

AERO-NEUROSIS

The sense of rootlessness and lack of direction after the Great War was common to those who were there. Even today historians and enthusiasts still wrestle with the meaning of the First World War. The ossuaries and vast cemeteries in Europe speak volumes as to the loss of life, but finding meaning in the loss is as varied and personal as those who fought. From the moment they decided to join up, they became heroes in my opinion. They made the conscious choice to help their country and their aspiration was to bring credit and honour to themselves, their squadrons, and their homeland. Each human being is composed of a unique blend of strengths, weaknesses and foibles. Each person is different, and each person had to endure a unique blend of circumstances during the Great War. For some it was a combination of machine guns, mud, barbed wire, and watching their friends get mowed down in trench warfare. For aviators it was different – not worse or better, just different. Each man responded to the crucible of war differently according to his or her latent and manifest qualities. It is entirely absurd and unfair to think that they all should come through this defining experience of their lives with grace, equanimity, and unscarred by what they experienced.

It was a bittersweet experience and transformation, defying easy explanation or quantification. On the one hand there were horrible moments that strained the sanity of these men; on the other, there was an excitement and intoxication about it that would not have been the same without the danger. Elliott White Springs said that:

> 'No matter where I go or what I do, the best part of me will always remain between Zeebrugge and Armentieres, and in front of Cambrai. There I lived a life, a long lifetime, there lie my companions, and many adversaries and there also lies the biggest part of myself.'[3]

Arthur Gould Lee reflecting on his flying experience after the war described loneliness, a sense of loss, patriotic rationalization, and mourning:

> 'Here at the corner of the chateau wall, in the sunshine, by the waving grain, with everything now at peace, I remembered them and was filled with a heavy sense of loneliness. I knew that although I had not been killed, something in me had. Something had gone out of me and was buried, and would always be buried, in a hundred cemeteries, in France and in

CONCLUSIONS

England, along with the companions of my youth who had died that our country might live.'[4]

Those who survived the war were forever changed by it. Their pre-1914 lives ceased to exist and when the guns fell silent, many who survived continued to struggle to carve out a productive and positive life as best they could. Some fared better than others.

It is also important to remember that those who fought in the Great War never envisaged there could be another. Their reasons for joining the fight were varied; some in the naiveté of youth craved adventure, some were idealists who felt they wanted to play a small part in making the world safe for civilization, the ultimate paradox – every 'civilized' nation contributed to the outbreak of the war. At the time of the Armistice a global feeling of hope was preponderant, and those that had survived the crucible of war would carry both the horrors and pleasures of war with them for the rest of their lives. Eddie Rickenbacker wrote at the time of the Armistice, 'How can one enjoy life without this highly spiced sauce of danger?' Those that perished did not have to bear this burden, but then again they gave the very flower of their youth; these men would not experience the joys of raising families, having productive careers, enjoying the twilight of their lives among loved ones.

Today, dozens of lovingly tended cemeteries, ossuaries, and memorials stretch across what was the Western Front. Many have ceremonies commemorating the dead such as the Last Post bell- ringing every night since 1928 at 8 pm at the Menin Gate, its melancholy tone affirming that we still remember and mourn. One hundred years has softened the Western Front but it can never fully heal nor should it; its lessons should always remain somewhat dissonant, compelling us to be always wary of the human factors that led to its genesis. The shattered remains of aircraft and other weapons of war have long since been removed or absorbed by the forgiving landscape, although munitions are still found and the scarred topography will never be as it was before the war. The fallen have been buried and memorialized, but the poppies still grow, just as vibrant and indifferently as they did in 1914, beckoning us to never forget what happened there.

Bibliography

ANDERSON, Graeme H. *The Medical and Surgical Aspects of Aviation*. London: Oxford University Press, 1919.

ARMSTRONG, Harry. *The Principles and Practices of Aviation Medicine*. Philadelphia: Williams & Wilkins Co., 1943,

BARKER, Pat. *Regeneration*. New York: The Penguin Group, 1992.

BEARD, James. *American Nervousness*. New York: G.P. Putnam's Sons, 1881.

BENNETT, Alan. *Captain Roy Brown, Vol. 1*. New York: Brick Tower Press, 2011.

BOGACZ, Ted. 'War Neurosis and Cultural Change in England 1914-22: The Work of the War Office Committee of Enquiry into 'Shell-Shock.' *Journal of Contemporary History*, Vol. 24, No. 2. pp. 227-256.

BORDEAUX, Henry. *Georges Guynemer—Knight of the Air*. New Haven: Yale University Press, 1918.

BOURKE, Joanna. *An Intimate History of Killing*. London: Granta Books, 1999.

BRONNENKANT, Lance. *Blue Max Airman Volume 8*. Reno: Aeronaut Books, 2016.

BROWN, Malcolm, '100 Years of Maxim's Killing Machine' *New York Times*, November 26, 1985.

BULL, Stephen. *German Machine guns of The First World War*. Oxford: Osprey Publishing, 2016.

CROUCH, Tom. *The Bishop's Boys*. New York: W.W. Norton & Co., 1989.

DAVIS, Burke. *Warbird*. Chapel Hill: The University of North Carolina Press, 1987.

FRIEDRICH, Bretislav. 'Fritz Haber (1868-1934)' *Angewandte Chemie (*International Edition) 44, (2005): 1-23.

GARROS, Roland. *Memoires*. Paris: Hachette Book Group, 1966.

GRIDER, John MacGavock. *Warbirds—Diary of an Unknown Aviator*. New York: George H. Doran Co., 1926.

BIBLIOGRAPHY

GUNN, Roger. *Raymond Collishaw and the Black Flight*. Toronto: Dundurn Press, 2013.

HALL, James N. *My Island Home*. Honolulu: Mutual Publishing Co., 2001.

HERRIS, Jack. *Aircraft of the First World War 1914-1918*. London: Amber Books Ltd., 2010.

JONES, Edgar, WESSELY, Simon. "Battle for the mind: World War 1 and the Birth of Military Psychiatry". The Lancet, Volume 384, Issue 9955 (2014), 1708-1714.

JUNGER, Ernst. *Storm of Steel*. London: Penguin Books Ltd., 1961.

LAMBERT, William. *Combat Report*. London: William Kimber & Co., 1973.

LEE, Arthur Gould. *Open Cockpit*. London: Jarrolds Publishers, 1969.

LEWIS, Cecil. *Sagittarius Rising*. New York: Harcourt, Brace & Co., 1936.

LINDBERGH, Charles. *The Spirit of St. Louis*. New York: Charles Scribner's Sons, 1953.

LOUGHRAN, Tracy. 'Shell Shock, Trauma, and the First World War: The Making of a Diagnosis and its Histories.' *Journal of the History of Medicine and Allied Sciences*, Volume 67, Number 1 (2010), 94-119.

MACLANACHAN, William. *Fighter Pilot*. Philadelphia: Casemate, 2015.

MANNOCK, Mick. *The Personal Diary of 'Mick' Mannock*. London: Neville Spearman Ltd., 1966.

MAXIM, Hiram. *My Life*. New York: McBride, Nast and Co., 1915.

McCUDDEN, James. *Flying Fury: Five Years in the Royal Flying Corps*. London: John Hamilton Ltd., 1918.

McMINNIES, W. G. *Practical Flying*. New York: George H. Doran Co., 1918.

MECHIN, David. 'Georges Guynemer.' *Cross and Cockade International* Vol. 43, no.3 (2012): 147-165.

MORTANE, Jacques. *Georges Guynemer*. New York: Moffat, Yard & Co., 1918.

PARSONS, Edwin. *I Flew with the Lafayette Escadrille*. Indianapolis: E.C. Seale & Co., 1937.

REED, Fiona. 'War Psychiatry,' *1914-1918 Online, International Encyclopaedia of the First World War*. Version 1.0, updated Jan. 8, 2017. 1-18.

REMARQUE, Erich M. *All Quiet on the Western Front*. New York: Random House, 1958.

RICKENBACKER, Edward. *Fighting the Flying Circus*. Garden City: Doubleday & Co., 1965.

RIVERS, W.H.R. 'The Repression of War Experience.' Delivered before the Section of Psychiatry, Royal Society of Medicine, on Dec. 4th, 1917, By W. H. R. Rivers, M.D.Lond., F.R.C.P. L., F.R.S., Late Medical Officer, Craig Lockhart War Hospital: 1-20.

ROUZEAU-AUDOIN, S; BECKER, Annette. *14-18 Understanding the Great War*. New York: Farrar, Straus, and Giroux, LLC, 2002.

SIMPSON, Colin. The Lusitania. Boston: Little, Brown and Co., 1972.

SMITH, Adrian. *Mick Mannock, Fighter Pilot*. London: Palgrave Macmillan Publishers, 2001.

SPRINGS, Elliott. *Letters from a War Bird*. Columbia: University of South Carolina Press, 2012,

UDET, Ernst. *Ace of the Black Cross*. London: Frontline Books, 2013.

WELLS, H.G. *The War in the Air*. London: George Bell & Sons, 1908.

WILMER, William H. *Aviation Medicine in the A.E.F*. Washington: Government Printing Office, 1920.

WOHL, Robert. *A Passion for Wings*. New Haven: Yale University Press, 1994.

Notes

Chapter 1
1. James Beard, *American Nervousness* (New York: G.P. Putnam's Sons, 1881), p. VI.
2. Stephen Bull, *German Machine guns of WWI* (Oxford: Osprey Publishing, 2016) p 8.
3. Malcolm Brown, '100 Years of Maxim's Killing Machine' *NY Times*, 1985.
4. Hiram Maxim, *My Life* (New York: McBride, Nast & Co. 1915) p. 170.
5. Ibid, p. 172.
6. Ibid, p. 179.
7. Maxim, *My Life*, p. 182.
8. Ibid, p. 219-220.
9. Ibid. p. 230.
10. Ibid, p. 258.
11. Maxim, *My Life*, p. 315.
12. Ibid, p. 316.
13. Robert Wohl, *Passion for Wings* (New Haven: Yale University Press, 1994), p. 9.
14. Bretislav Friedrich, 'Fritz Haber (1868-1934)' p. 2.
15. Ibid.
16. Colin Simpson, *The Lusitania* (Boston: Little, Brown & Co. 1972), p. 31.
17. Ibid.
18. H. G. Wells, *War in the Air*, (London: George Bell & Sons, 1908), p. 103.
19. Ibid, 106.
20. Comment made by Edward, Viscount Grey of Fallodon, August 3, 1914, while standing at the window of his room in the British Foreign Office, London, as the lamplighters were going about their rounds in St. James Park.

Chapter 2
1. Wells, *War in the Air*, pp. 17-18.
2. Tom Crouch, *Bishop's Boys* (New York: W.W. Norton & Co. 1989) p. 364.

3. Wohl, *Passion for Wings*, p. 69.
4. Wohl, *Passion*, p. 107.
5. Wells, *War in the Air*, pp. 73-74.
6. Cecil Lewis, *Sagittarius Rising*, (New York: Harcourt, Brace & Co., 1936), p. 111.
7. Ibid, p.135.
8. James N. Hall, *My Island Home* (Honolulu: Mutual Publishing Co. 2001) p. 177.
9. Ibid, p. 225.
10. Arthur Lee, *Open Cockpit* (London: Jarrolds Publishers, 1969) p. 58.
11. Charles Lindbergh, *Spirit of St. Louis*. (New York: Charles Scribner's Sons, 1953), p. 12.

Chapter 3
1. Wohl, *Passion*. P. 15.
2. Ibid.
3. Ibid. P. 17.
4. Wohl, *Passion*. P. 18.
5. Ibid.
6. Ibid, p. 38.
7. Ibid. p. 42. The 14bis was an aircraft of Dumont's own design based largely on the Voisin biplane p. 41 Tom Crouch noted the distance as being 726 feet in 21 3/5 seconds. *Bishop's Boys*, p. 317.
8. Ibid.
9. Wohl, *Passion*. P. 19.
10. Flint sold weapons and technology to anyone who could pay the price—'on one occasion he purchased, equipped, and armed an entire fleet for a South American country on a merchant of death then ever there was one who made fortunes from the anxieties generated by a constantly escalating arms race among the world's great and would be powers.' Wohl, Passion, p. 20. *Bishop's Boys*, p. 328.
11. Crouch, *Bishop's Boys*, p. 329.
12. Ibid. p. 330.
13. Ibid, p. 44.
14. Ibid.
15. Wohl, *Passion*, p. 45.
16. Crouch, *Bishops Boys*, p. 377.
17. Ibid. p. 385.
18. Wohl, *Passion*. P. 21.
19. Wohl, p. 48.

NOTES

20. Ibid, p. 54.
21. Ibid.
22. Crouch, *Bishop's Boys*, p. 399.
23. Ibid.
24. Wohl, *Passion*, p. 57.
25. Ibid, p. 59.
26. Ibid.
27. Ibid.
28. Ibid, p. 61.
29. Ibid, p. 65.
30. Lewis, *Sagittarius Rising* (New York: Harcourt, Brace & Co., 1936), p. 116.
31. John Herris, *Aircraft of The First World War* (London: Amber Books Ltd., 2010), p. 16.

Chapter 4

1. Lewis, *Sagittarius*, p. 84.
2. Joanna Bourke, *Intimate History of Killing* (London: Granta Books, 1999), p. 65.
3. https://www.britannica.com/event/Franco-German-War
4. Encyclopedia Britannica.
5. Erich Remarque, *All Quiet on the Western Front* (New York: Random House, 1958), pp. 274-75.
6. Ibid. p. 286.
7. Lewis, *Sagittarius*, p. 89.
8. http://www.bbc.co.uk/history/worldwars/wwone/nonflash_tank.shtml
9. Lewis, *Sagittarius*, p. 90.
10. http://www.vlib.us/the First World War/resources/archives/texts/uboatu9.html, original document is in the Royal Navy Submarine Museum and was published in: *Submarines and the War at Sea, 1914-1918*, written by Richard Compton-Hall, 1991, MacMillan.

Chapter 5

1. Adrian Smith, *Mick Mannock* (London: Palgrave Macmillan Publishers, 2001), p. 136.
2. Ibid, p. 135.
3. Ibid, p. 136. Leed wrote *Noman's Land*.
4. William MacLanachan, *Fighter Pilot*, (Philadelphia: Casemate, 2015) pp. 49-50.
5. Ernst Udet, *Ace of the Black Cross* (London: Frontline Books, 2013) p. 63.

6. Lewis, *Sagittarius*, pp. 136-7.
7. Edward Rickenbacker, *Fighting the Flying Circus* (Garden City: Doubleday & Co.,1965), p. 194.
8. Arthur Lee, *Open Cockpit*. P. 180-81.
9. Ibid, p. 181.
10. Arthur Lee, *Open Cockpit*. P. 182.
11. Adrian Smith, *Mannock, Fighter Pilot*, p. 136.
12. Jacques Mortane, *Guynemer* (New York: Moffat, Yard & Co., 1918) p. 1307-22 (kindle edition).

Chapter 6
1. Graeme Anderson, *Medical and Surgical Aspects of Aviation* (Oxford: Oxford University Press, 1919) p. 96.
2. Ibid.
3. Ibid. p. 97.
4. 'In order to study the psychology of flying, the medical officer should have experience of the air, preferably as a passenger. He who would probe the subject more deeply can only do so by having piloted an aeroplane by himself. One does not advocate that all R.A.F. medical officers should learn to fly, but the interest in their work will be heightened by making occasional passenger flights.' P. 70.
5. Simon Wessley, Edgar Jones, 'Battle for the Mind,' p. 1708. Mott was director of the London County Council's pathology laboratory at Claybury Asylum.
6. Ibid. p. 1709. Myers was a consulting psychologist to the British Expeditionary Force—he observed soldiers in combat at the Western Front. In late 1915 he would modify his definition by stating that a shell burst was simply the 'last straw' to an already worn out nervous system.
7. Ibid.
8. Ibid.
9. Ted Bogacz, 'War Neurosis and Cultural Change in England,' p. 228.
10. Loughran stated that'During the war, shell shock was understood in many different ways: as a psychological reaction to war, as a type of concussion, or as a physiological response to prolonged fear.'p. 107.
11. Ibid, p. 1712.
12. Fiona Reid, 'War Psychiatry,' p. 8.
13. Bogacz, 'War Neurosis,' p. 228.
14. http://www.vlib.us/medical/CCS/ccs.htm
15. Jones, Wessely, *Lancet*. P. 1710.
16. Bogacz, 'War Neurosis,'p. 235.
17. Rivers, 'The Repression of War Experience,' p. 5.

NOTES

18. Ibid, p. 6.
19. Ibid.
20. Lee, *Open Cockpit*, p. 60.
21. Bourke, *An Intimate History*, p. 212.
22. Fiona Reed, 'War Psychiatry,' p. 5.
23. Roland Garros, *Memoires (*Paris: Hachette, 1966), p. 260.
24. Wohl, *Passion*, p. 208.
25. Ibid, p. 210.
26. Remarque, *All Quiet*, p. 263.
27. Remarque, *All Quiet*, p. 88.
28. John Grider, *Warbirds* (New York: George H. Doran Co., 1926), p. 267.
29. Pat Barker, *Regeneration* (New York: The Penguin Group, 1992), p. 184.
30. Edwin Parsons, *I Flew with the Lafayette Escadrille* (Indianapolis: E.C. Seale & Co., 1937) p. 215.
31. Ibid, p. 213-14.
32. Lewis, *Sagittarius*. p. 50.
33. Lee, *Open Cockpit*, p. 70.
34. Alan Bennett, *Roy Brown* (New York: Brick Tower Press, 2011), pp, 564-5.
35. W.G. McMinnies, *Notes on Practical Flying* (New York: George H. Doran Co., 1918), pp. 216-17.
36. Tracy Loughran, 'Shell Shock, Trauma, and WWI,' p. 95.

Chapter 7
1. Bourke, *An Intimate History*, p. 72.
2. Elliott Springs, *Letters from a War Bird* (Columbia: University of South Carolina Press, 2012), p. XIII.
3. Ibid, p. XV.
4. Spring, *Letters*, p. XVI.
5. Ibid, p. 62.
6. Ibid, p. 82.
7. Springs, *Letters*, p. 82. Vaughan surmised it was a Pup he was having difficulty with, but I believe it was the Spad—which required a fast take-off and landing. He was flying Spads on Feb 11th according to his log which also notes 'roll my wheels at 114 mph' suggesting the high speeds required to land and ascend in a Spad.
8. Ibid, pp. 88-89.
9. Ibid, p. 130.
10. Ibid, p. 145.
11. Springs, *Letters*. P. 152.

12. Springs, *Letters,* p. 147.
13. Ibid. p. 149.
14. Ibid, p. 160.
15. Ibid, p. 161.
16. Ibid, p. 162.
17. Ibid, p. 163.
18. Ibid, p. 166.
19. Ibid, p. 170.
20. Springs, *Letters.* P. 171.
21. Ibid.
22. Ibid, p. 174.
23. His relapse was due to poisoned/spoiled medication.
24. Ibid, p. 175.
25. P. 182.
26. Bourke, *Intimate History*, p. 245.
27. Ibid, p. 182-83
28. Ibid, p. 184-5.
29. Ibid, p. 187.
30. Springs, *Letters*, p. 210.
31. Ibid, p. 225.
32. Ibid, p. 177.
33. Ibid, p. 178.
34. Springs, *Letters*, p. 179.
35. Ibid, p. 180.
36. Ibid.
37. Springs, Letters, p. 189-90.
38. Ibid, p. 193.
39. Ibid, p. 194.
40. Ibid, p. 195.
41. Ibid, pp 196-7.
42. Springs, *Letters*, p. 198.
43. Rickenbacker, *Fighting the Flying Circus*, p. 172.
44. Springs*, Letters*, pp. 199-200.
45. Ibid, p. 201.
46. Ibid, p. 202.
47. Ibid.
48. Ibid, p. 204.
49. Ibid, p. 207.
50. Ibid, p. 208.

NOTES

51. Ibid, pp. 208-9.
52. Ibid, p. 209.
53. Ibid, p. 211.
54. Springs, *Letters*, 212.
55. Ibid. p. 214.
56. Ibid, p. 215.
57. Ibid, p. 216.
58. Ibid.
59. Ibid, p. 217.
60. Springs, *Letters*, p. 220.
61. Ibid, p. 221.
62. Ibid, p. 222.
63. Ibid, p. 225.
64. Springs, *Letters*, p. 231.
65. Ibid, p. 239.
66. Ibid, p. 241.
67. Ibid, p. 240.
68. Springs, *Letters*, p. 242.
69. Ibid, pp 242-3.
70. Ibid, p. 249.
71. Ibid, p. 247.
72. Ibid, p. 250.
73. Ibid, pp 248-9.
74. Ibid, p. 269.
75. Ibid, p. 272.
76. John Grider, *Warbirds*, p. 14.
77. Ibid, p. 142.
78. Grider, *Warbirds*, pp. 174-5.
79. Ibid, p. 175.
80. Ibid, p. 187.
81. Springs, *Letters*, p. 239.
82. Grider, *Warbirds*, pp 204-5.
83. Ibid, p. 206.
84. Springs, *Letters*, p. 207.
85. Grider, *Warbirds*, p. 243.
86. Ibid, p. 253.
87. Ibid, p. 254.
88. Ibid, p. 261.
89. Grider, *Warbirds*, p. 261.

90. Ibid, p. 264.
91. Ibid, p. 267.
92. Grider, *Warbirds*, p. 269.
93. Ibid, p. 271.
94. Ibid.
95. Burke Davis, *Warbird* (Chapel Hill: The University of North Carolina Press, 1987), pp 170-171.

Chapter 8
1. William Lambert, *Combat Report* (London: William Kimber & Co., 1973), P. 140.
2. Harry Armstrong, *Principles and Practices of Aviation Medicine*. (Philadelphia: Williams & Wilkins Co., 1943), p. 400.
3. Ibid, p. 145.
4. Lambert, *Combat Report*, p. 149.
5. Ibid, p. 155.
6. Lambert, *Combat Report*. Pp. 158-9.
7. Ibid, p. 166.
8. Ibid, p. 201-202.
9. Lambert, *Combat Report*, p. 202.
10. Armstrong, *Principles and Practice*, p. 419.
11. Ibid, p. 203.
12. Ibid, p. 218.
13. Ibid, p. 222.
14. Ibid, p. 227.
15. Ibid, p. 231.
16. Lambert, *Combat Report*, p. 232.
17. Ibid, p. 237.
18. Ibid, p. 247-48.
19. Ibid, p. 248-9. Lambert's memory loss for this period could be attributed to electro-shock treatment as short term memory loss is a side-effect of this type of treatment.
20. Ibid, p. 249.

Chapter 9
1. Alan Bennett, *Roy Brown*, p. 48.
2. Ibid, p. 60.
3. Ibid, p. 64.
4. Ibid, p. 71.
5. Bennett, *Roy Brown*, pp. 79-80.

NOTES

6. Ibid, p. 88.
7. Ibid, p. 150.
8. Ibid, p. 151.
9. Ibid, p. 166.
10. Ibid, p. 181.
11. Ibid, p. 221.
12. Bennett, *Brown*, p. 229.
13. Ibid, p. 238.
14. Ibid, p. 247.
15. Ibid. p. 260-- Flight leader was usually reserved for higher ranks than Brown's sub-lieutenant status.
16. Ibid, p. 275.
17. Ibid, p. 277.
18. Ibid, p. 281.
19. Ibid, p. 282.
20. Bennett, *Brown*, p. 283-4.
21. Ibid, p. 287.
22. Ibid, p. 323.
23. Ibid, p. 331. It should be noted that there were roughly as many training accident deaths as combat one flying the Camel. Another noteworthy fact—the C of G was imperfectly understood during this period. Had the planes been balanced properly they would have been far easier to handle. It should also be noted that pilots flying Camels shot down 1294 aircraft between June 1917 and November 1918—more than any other type of aircraft. P. 331.
24. Ibid. sung to the tune of 'Oh, where, oh where has my little dog gone?'
25. Ibid, p. 332.
26. Ibid, p. 333.
27. Ibid, p. 339-40.
28. Ibid, p. 351.
29. Ibid, p. 355.
30. Ibid. p. 402. His friend Stearne accompanied him.
31. Ibid. p. 404.
32. Early Dr. 1's suffered from wing failures due to shoddy workmanship or substandard materials.
33. Bennett, Brown, p. 434.
34. Ibid, p. 449.
35. Bennet, *Brown*, p. 479. Pilot of this Dr. 1 was Georg Wolff of Jasta 6 p. 480. This was a shared victory with Lt. F.J.W. Mellersh; it was Roy's eighth victory.

AERO-NEUROSIS

36. Ibid, p. 481. This was the last time Roy would ever eat rabbit for the rest of his life! P. 482.
37. Roger Gunn, *Raymond Collishaw and the Black Flight* (Toronto: Dundurn Press, 2013), p. 177.
38. Bennett, *Brown,* p. 492.
39. Bennett, *Brown*, p. 492.
40. Ibid, p. 494.
41. Ibid, p. 496.
42. Ibid. p. 498.
43. From a letter to Roy Brown's mother.
44. Bennett, *Brown*, p. 500.
45. Ibid, p. 501.
46. Ibid, p. 512.
47. Ibid, p. 513.
48. Bennett, *Brown*, p. 513.
49. Bourke, *Intimate History*, p. 239.
50. Ibid, p. 523.
51. Ibid, pp. 564-5.
52. Ibid, p. 565. In December 1917 the Mount Vernon buildings became the Royal Flying Corps Central Hospital. In March 1918 an Air Medical Investigation Committee was established to investigate the problems of special disabilities associated with flying, especially anoxaemia (oxygen deficiency) caused by flying at high altitudes.
53. Bennett, *Brown*, p. 589.
54. Ibid, p. 653.

Chapter 10

1. Udet, *Ace of the Black Cross* (London: Frontline Books, 2013), p. XI of preface.
2. Bourke, *Intimate History*, p. 96.
3. Ibid, p. 5.
4. Ibid, p. 25.
5. Udet, *Black Cross*, p. 31.
6. Carter Fox,'The Gallipoli fighter,'*Flightpath*, p. 2.
7. Immelmann turn: steep climb followed by sharp rudder input–in effect the modern 'stall-turn.'
8. Ibid, p. 32.
9. Ibid, P. 35.
10. Ibid, p. 36.
11. Bourke, *Intimate History*, 'Slaughter could be likened to an orgasmic, charismatic experience. However you looked at it, war was a 'turn on." P. 3.

NOTES

'Combat imparted a sense of tremendous power…people could take an immense delight in breaking the highest moral law.' P. 20.
12. Ibid, p. 39.
13. Ibid, p. 50.
14. Lance Bronnenkant, *Blue Max Airmen Vol. 8* (Aeronaut Books, 2016), p. 12.
15. Ibid, p. 14.
16. Udet, *Ace of Black Cross*, p. 50.
17. Ibid, p. 50-51.
18. Ibid, p. 54-55.
19. Udet, *Ace of the Black Cross*, p. 55.
20. Ibid, p. 56.
21. Ibid, 56-7.
22. Ibid, 57-58.
23. Udet, *Ace of the Black Cross*, pp 60-63.
24. Ibid, p. 70.
25. Ibid, pp 70-71.
26. Ibid, p. 102.
27. Ibid, p. 74.
28. Udet, *Ace of the Black Cross*, p. 74.
29. Ibid.
30. Lee, *Open Cockpit*, pp. 175-76.
31. Ibid, p. 81.
32. Udet, *Ace of the Black Cross*, pp 81-82.
33. Ibid, p. 90.
34. Ibid, pp 90-91.
35. Udet, *Ace of the Black Cross*, p. 97-98.
36. Ibid, p. 102.
37. Ibid, p. 103.
38. Ibid, p.121.
39. Ibid,. p. 122.
40. Udet, *Ace of the Black Cross*. P. 126.
41. Ibid, p. 192.
42. Ishoven, Bowers, *Fall of an Eagle*.

Chapter 11
1. Mick Mannock, *The Personal Diary of Mick Mannock* (London: Neville Spearman Ltd., 1966), p. 11.
2. Ibid.
3. Ibid, p. 12.
4. Ibid.

5. Ibid, p. 13.
6. Smith, *Mick Mannock Fighter Pilot*, p. 88.
7. Ibid, p. 19.
8. Smith, *Mick M. Fighter Pilot*. P18-19.
9. Ibid.
10. Mannock, *Diary,* p. 12.
11. Ibid, pp 12-13.
12. Mannock, *Diary*, p. 14.
13. Ibid, p. 15.
14. Ibid, p. 15.
15. Ibid, p. 16.
16. Ibid.
17. Ibid, p. 17.
18. Ibid, p.18.
19. Ibid, p. 20.
20. Smith, *Mick Mannock*, p. 59.
21. Ibid.
22. Ibid, p. 58.
23. Mannock, *Diary*, p. 20.
24. Ibid, p. 21.
25. Smith, *MM figher pilot*, p. 57.
26. Ibid, p.62.
27. Ibid, p. 22-23.
28. James McCudden. *Flying Fury: Five Years in the Royal Flying Corps* (Philadelphia: Casemate, 2015), p. 131.
29. Mannock, *Diary*. P. 24.
30. Ibid, p. 31.
31. Smith, *MM Fighter pilot*, p. 69.
32. Ibid, p. 33-34.
33. Ibid, p. 70.
34. Ibid, p. 45-47.
35. Oughton, *Diary*, p. 153.
36. Mannock, *Diary,* p. 49.
37. Smith, *MM figher pilot*, p. 72.
38. Oughton, *Diary,* p. 154.
39. Ibid, p. 157.
40. Ibid.
41. Mannock, *Diary,* p. 69.
42. Mannock, *Diary*, p. 158.

NOTES

43. Rivers, 'The Repression of War Experience,' pp. 13-14.
44. Nieuports were unsuited for close ground support—they could not carry bombs, were slow, and lightly built. Thus were easily damaged at low altitudes. Sopwith Pups were similarly handicapped. Spad VIIs flown by the RFC fared better.
45. Ernst Junger, *Storm of Steel* (London: Penguin Books Ltd., 1961), p.133.
46. Mannock, *Diary*, p. 69.
47. Smith, *MM fighter pilot*. P. 60.
48. Ibid, p. 71.
49. Oughton, *Diary*, p. 158.
50. Bronnenkant, *Blue Max Airman*, p. 70.
51. Ibid, p. 71.
52. A term that gained preponderance in the RAF during the First World War..
53. Mannock, *Diary,* p. 75.
54. Ibid, p. 84-85.
55. Ibid. p. 159.
56. Mannock, *Diary*, p. 111.
57. Ibid, p. 113.
58. Bourke, *Intimate History*, p. 212.
59. Ibid, p. 115.
60. Ibid, p. 117,119.
61. Ibid, p. 164.
62. Ibid, p. 119.
63. Mannock, *Diary.* P. 129.
64. Franks, Norman; Bailey, Frank W.; Guest, Russell. *Above the Lines: The Aces and Fighter Units of the German Air Service, Naval Air Service and Flanders Marine Corps*, 1914–1918. Grub Street, 1993 p. 72.
65. Mannock, *Diary*, p. 137.
66. Ibid, p. 139.
67. Ibid, p. 168.
68. Ibid, p. 143.
69. Mannock, *Diary,* p. 171-172.
70. Ibid, p. 173. The cat was renamed 'Fiddle' in pleasant company.
71. Ibid.
72. Ibid, P. 174.
73. Ibid, p. 175.
74. Mannock, *Diary,* p. 189.
75. Ibid, p. 176.
76. Ibid, p. 178.

77. Ibid, p. 179.
78. Ibid, p. 181.
79. Ibid. p. 182.
80. Ibid.
81. Smith, *Mannock fighter pilot*, p. 104.
82. Ibid. p. 184.
83. Ibid, p. 185.
84. Ibid. p. 186.
85. Smith, *Mannock fighter pilot*. P. 112. Oughton noted that he 'left the mess in disgust' rather than take part in a toast to Richthofen.'
86. Mannock, *Diary*, p. 187.
87. Dudgeon, *Mick*, p. 132.
88. Mannock, *Diary*, p. 188.
89. Ibid, p. 189.
90. Ibid, pp 189-90.
91. Ibid, p. 191.
92. Ibid, p. 193.
93. Ibid, p. 192.
94. Smith, *Mannock Fighter pilot*, p. 113-4.
95. Mannock, *Diary*, p. 193.
96. Smith, *Mannock Fighter pilot*. P. 113.
97. Ibid, p. 120.
98. Ibid.
99. Mannock, *Diary*, p. 194.
100. Smith, *Mannock fighter pilot*. P. 120.
101. Mannock, *Diary*, p. 195.
102. Smith, p. 120.
103. Ibid, p. 196.
104. Ibid.
105. Smith, p. 96.
106. Ibid, p. 196-7.
107. Ibid, p. 197.
108. Smith, p. 118.
109. Ibid, p. 155.
110. Ibid, p. 156.
111. Mannock, *Diary*, pp. 197-98.
112. Ibid, p. 198.
113. Ibid, pp 199-200. Smith, p. 127.
114. Smith, P. 127-28.

NOTES

115. Smith, *Mannock fighter pilot*, p. 121.
116. Ibid.
117. Ibid.
118. Report by E.W. Craig. *Army Report of the War Committee of Enquiry into Shell Shock*. 1922, p 86-7.
119. Smith, p.134.
120. Ibid, p. 137.

Chapter 12

1. Henry Bordeaux, *Georges Guynemer—Knight of the Air* (New Haven: Yale University Press, 1918), P. 11.
2. Boudreaux, *Guynemer*, p. 33.
3. Bordeaux, p. 22.
4. Ibid, p. 26-7.
5. Ibid, p. 28.
6. Ibid, pp. 28-9.
7. David Mechin, 'Georges Guynemer' *Cross and Cockade International* Vol. 43 p. 147.
8. Bordeaux. P. 31.
9. Ibid, p. 32. During his college years he played wargames with his friends.
10. Ibid, p. 35.
11. Bordeaux, *Guynemer*, p. 47-8.
12. Ibid, p. 49.
13. Ibid, pp 54-55.
14. Ibid, p. 59.
15. Ibid, p. 60.
16. Ibid, p. 61.
17. Ibid, p. 62.
18. A Penguin was a Bleriot XI with clipped wings—it could taxi only which was precisely the point for students.
19. Mechin, 'Georges Guynemer', p. 148.
20. Bordeaux, *Guynemer*, p. 63.
21. Bordeaux, p. 71.
22. Mechin, *Georges G.* p. 148.
23. Ibid, p. 149.
24. Ibid. he was flying a single seat conversion of the two-seater Nieuport X.
25. Ibid, p. 81.
26. Mechin, p. 149. The abrupt dive was caused presumably by the pilot slumping forward on the stick.

27. Bordeaux, *Guynemer*, p. 91.
28. Ibid.
29. Ibid, p. 94-5.
30. Mechin, *Guynemer*, p. 149.
31. Ibid, p. 150.
32. Ibid, p. 151.
33. Ibid.
34. Mechin, *Guynemer*, p. 153.
35. Ibid.
36. Ibid, p. 154.
37. Ibid.
38. Ibid, p. 155.
39. Ibid.
40. Ibid.
41. Mechin, *Guynemer,* p. 155.
42. Ibid, p. 156.
43. Ibid. p. 157.
44. Ibid.
45. Ibid.
46. Ibid, p. 161.
47. Mechin, *Guynemer*, p. 161.
48. Ibid. p. 162.
49. Ibid.
50. Ibid.
51. Ibid.
52. Mortane, *Ace of Aces*, p.1348-52.
53. Ibid.
54. Mechen, *Guynemer*, p. 164.
55. Mortane, *Ace,* 1946-48.
56. Ibid, p.

Conclusions
1. Lee, *Open Cockpit*, p 194.
2. Remarque, *All Quiet*, p. 294.
3. Springs, *Letters from a Warbird*, p. 272.
4. Lee, *Open Cockpit*, p.210.

Index

Aircraft
  Albatros D. III 76, 112, 114
  Albatros DV 66
  Aviatik, type B 89, 129, 130
  Avro, aircraft 74
  Bleriot XI, monoplane 18, 74, 128, 157
  DFW, two-seater aircraft 113, 133
  Flyer, Wrights 9, 13-16, 27, 74
  Fokker D. VII 36, 46-50, 52-55, 63, 71, 102, 116
  Fokker Dr. 1, triplane 72, 79, 80, 82, 86, 98, 116
  Golden Flier, Curtiss 17
  LVG, two-seater aircraft 123
  Nieuport, aircraft 75, 108, 109, 111, 114, 115, 129-131
  Pfalz D. III, aeroplane 71, 114, 118
  Rumpler Taube 18
  S.E 5a, aeroplane 42, 45, 48, 115, 117, 123
  Sopwith Camel, aeroplane 45, 47, 48, 54, 77-79, 81, 85, 151
  Sopwith Pup, aeroplane 25, 42, 75-77, 147
  Sopwith triplane 76, 112, 133
  Spad, aeroplane 42, 95, 96, 131, 133, 135, 147
  Wright Model B 4, 74

Airfields
  Bertangles 80, 83
  Remaisnil 49
Alcohol, coping mechanism 35, 36, 38, 124
All Quiet on the Western Front 20, 21, 34, 37, 101, 121
Anderson, Graeme, Dr. 29, 36, 37, 38, 85
Armistice 11, 30, 57,
Annouellin Cemetery 112
Armstrong, Henry 66

Ball, Albert, Capt. 27, 28, 106, 111
Barker, William 27
Bartlett, F.C. 123
Battles
  Arras 111
  Omdurman 3
  Somme, offensive 31, 131
Beard, James 1, 88
Bechereau, Louis 131
Bennett, Alan 76, 81, 86
Bernard-Theirry, Capt. 128, 133
Bertraub, Joachim von 113, 114
Big Bertha 5, 20
Bishop, Billy 27, 42, 47, 53, 58, 115, 120, 121
Bishop, John Peale 40
Blaxland, Lionel 108

Bleriot, Louis ix, 9, 13, 16-18, 88
Bleyle, Inge 103
Bloody April 75, 76, 111
Boelcke, Oswald 26, 28, 34, 125
Bogacz, Ted 30
Bordeaux, Henry 126, 128, 129
Bourke, Joanna 20, 33, 46, 113
Brocard, Antonin 129
Brown, A. Roy vii, x, 32, 37,
   73-87, 100, 110, 123, 132, 137

Caldwell, Keith 'Grid' 118, 119
Callahan, Larry 41, 42, 47, 53, 54, 58
Canterbury viii, 104, 105
Carter, Andrew 89-91
Chanute, Octave 4, 8, 15
Churchill, Winston 5, 22, 124
Clausewitz, Carl von 24
Clay, Henry 49
Cole, Edwin 27
Collishaw, Raymond 80
Colyner, Wilfred T. 40
Compiegne viii, 127-130, 134
Constantinople 3, 108
Craig, E.W. 123
Crouch, Tom 26
Curtis, Kent 52
Curtiss, Glenn 1, 9, 17, 74, 88

Delagrange, Leon 16
Delporte, Maurice 132
Dumont, Santos 4, 9, 14-16

Eyles, Jim 105, 109, 111, 120

Fisch, Rene 131

Garros, Roland 9, 33
Gas, poison 5, 21, 23, 24, 72

General Airways Ltd. 87
German Air Service 88, 89
Glinkermann, Willy 95, 96
Gontermann, Heinrich 93, 94
Goring, Hermann 92, 102, 103
Grider, John M. vii, 34, 41-44, 48,
   50, 58-60, 62, 64, 65
Gussmann, Siegfried 99
Guynemer, George viii, 26, 28, 32,
   95, 96, 97, 106, 125-135
Guynemer, Paul 126

Haber, Fritz 5
Hall, James N. 11, 52
Hanisch, Puz 94-96
Heurtaux, Alfred 131, 132
Hospitals
   Craiglockhart 31, 32
   Duchess of Sutherland 45
   General Hospital, 24 RAF 37
   General, RAF 85
   Queen Alexandra's Hospital 72
Hypoxia 32, 84

Immelmann, Max 26, 28, 34, 80,
   91, 131
Inglis, Donald 122

Jonas, Lucien H. 126
Jones, Ira 'Taffy' 110, 117-119,
   121
Junger, Ernst 111

Kill Devil Hills 4

Lambert, Charles de 16
Lambert, William vii, 38, 54, 63,
   66-72, 98, 123
Langley, Samuel P. 4

INDEX

Latham, Hubert 16, 17
Le Mans 9, 15
Lee, Arthur Gould 12, 25, 27, 32, 37, 57, 99, 136, 138
Leed, Eric 25, 28
Levavasseur, Leon R. 5
Lewis, Cecil 10, 11, 18, 21-23, 26, 36
Lilienthal, Otto 8
Lindbergh, Charles 12
London Colney 42, 116
Ludendorf, General 48
Lufbery, Raoul 26

MacCurdy, J.T. 123
Machine gun 2, 4, 18, 19, 23, 25, 45, 51, 79, 89, 97, 112, 138
MacLenachan, William, 'McScotch' 114-116
Mannock, Edward 'Mick' viii, 26, 27, 33, 34, 39, 42, 47, 53, 54, 61, 63, 64, 76, 86, 98, 99, 104-124, 131
Mannock, Julia 104, 105
Mannock, Patrick 105
Mark I, tank, British 22
Massdorp, C.R. 100
May, Lieutenant 81, 82
McCudden, James 27, 107, 121
McCurdy, John T. 84
McDonald, E. C. 40
Moran, Charles 33
Morane Parasol, Type L 129, 130
Mortanes, Jacques 26, 28, 106, 126, 130, 132, 133, 134
Mott, Frederick 29, 146
Myers, C.S. 29, 30, 146

Neurasthenia 1, 29, 31, 42, 63, 88
Newhall, Morton 46
Nungesser, Charles 132

Operation Michael 66, 79
Oughton, Frederick 109-111, 113, 114, 122

Parsons, Edwin 35, 36
Popkin, Cedric 81, 83
Prussianism ix, 92, 122

Remarque, Erich Maria 20, 3, 64, 101, 137
Rex, Hillary 63
Richthofen, Lothar von 111, 112
Richthofen, Manfred von 26, 28, 44, 53, 72, 80-83, 87, 97, 98, 100, 101, 111, 112, 119, 125
Rickenbacker, Eddie 26, 50, 135
Rivers, William H.R. 30-32, 43, 86, 110, 111, 120
Roy, Jules 132
Royal Air Force 37, 70, 79, 80, 82, 84, 86, 87
Royal Army Medical Corps 31
Royal Army Service Corps 31
Royal Engineers 31, 106
Royal Flying Corps 27, 68, 75, 78, 79, 107, 110-112
Royal Naval Air Service 73, 75, 78, 79

Santos-Dumont, Alberto 4, 9, 14-16
Selfredge, Thomas 16
Shell-shock x, 23, 29-31, 35
Shepard, Ben 39
Smallways, Bert 6, 9
Smith, Adrian 25, 104, 106, 123
Springs, Elliott W. vii, 34, 40-68, 70, 78, 80, 98, 120, 123, 138

Springs, Frances 65
Springs, Lena 40, 41, 44, 55
Springs, Leroy 40, 41, 45, 46, 54, 55, 57, 59, 60, 65
Squadrons
  Aero 17 45
  Aero 148 45, 48
  Escadrille Americaine 11, 26, 129, 131
  Jasta 11 53, 97, 98, 111
  24 66
  40 108, 114, 115
  74 116, 118, 119, 121
  85 42, 47, 58, 120-122
  209 80
St. Omer, France 44, 108, 112
Strafing, of troops 44, 48, 51, 52, 54, 66, 68, 70, 80, 98

Technology shock ix, 136
Thomas, Meredith, Capt. 107
Tilney, Leonard, Maj. 115
Tomkins, Eric 106
Trench warfare 19, 20, 24, 25, 39, 48, 113, 137, 138
Trenchard, Hugh, General 27, 106, 111, 115

Udet, Ernst ix, x, 26, 36, 38, 63, 64, 88, 89, 91-103, 110, 120
US Army Signal Corps 9, 13, 15-17, 58

Vaillet, Marcel 128
Vaughan, David 48, 147
Vedrines, Charles 129, 130
Verne, Jules 5, 23

Warbirds, Diary of an Unknown Aviator 58-63, 65
Warfare, mechanized vii, 24, 29-31, 136, 137
Western Front ix, 11, 12, 20, 30, 48, 66, 73, 126, 136
White, Grace Alison 40
Wignolle, Yvonne 132
Wilhelm II ix, 15
Wilson, Woodrow 6, 7, 62
Wohl, Robert 14, 33
Wright School of Aviation 74
Wright, Orville 12, 13
Wright, Wilbur 9, 15, 16

Zeppelins, dirigibles 23, 39, 73, 75, 136